Following the example of music publication, Source Books in Architecture offers an alternative to the traditional architectural monograph. If one is interested in hearing music, he or she simply purchases the desired recording. If, however, one wishes to study a particular piece in greater depth, it is possible to purchase the score— the written code that more clearly articulates the structure, organization, and creative process that brings the work into being. This series is offered in the same spirit. Each Source Book focuses on a single work by a particular architect or on a special topic in contemporary architecture. The work is documented with sketches, models, renderings, working drawings, and photographs at a level of detail that allows careful and thorough study of the project from its conception to the completion of design and construction.

The graphic component is accompanied by commentary from the architect and critics that further explores both the technical and cultural content of the work in question.

Source Books in Architecture was conceived by Jeffrey Kipnis and Robert Livesey and is the product of the Herbert Baumer seminars, a series of interactions between students and seminal practitioners at the Knowlton School of Architecture at The Ohio State University. After a significant amount of research on distinguished architects, students lead a discussion that encourages those architects to reveal their architectural motivations and techniques. The students record and transcribe the meetings, which become the basis of these Source Books.

The seminars are made possible by a generous bequest from Herbert Herndon Baumer. Educated at the Ecole des Beaux-Arts, Baumer was a professor in the Department of Architecture at The Ohio State University from 1922 to 1956. He had a dual career as a distinguished design professor who inspired many students and a noted architect who designed several buildings at The Ohio State University and other Ohio colleges.

Other Source Books in Architecture:
Morphosis/Diamond Ranch High School
The Light Construction Reader
Bernard Tschumi/Zénith de Rouen

ACKNOWLEDGMENTS

Working with Ben van Berkel and Caroline Bos, both in Columbus and in Amsterdam, has been a pleasure. I thank them for their thoroughgoing commitment to the project. Thanks are due as well to the staff at UN Studio, especially Machteld Kors, Ger Gijzen, and Ineke van der Burg, for their cheerful assistance, thoughtful insights, and warm hospitality. The generosity of Hans-Jürgen Commerell, who provided the wonderful construction photographs throughout this volume, also deserves special mention.

Robert Livesey, director of the Knowlton School of Architecture, continues to encourage and support the Source Books team in countless ways. As always, the advice of friends and colleagues, including George Acock, Mike Cadwell, Jackie Gargus, Carolyn Hank, José Oubrerie, Mike Meehan, Ted Musielewicz, Ryan Palider, Andrew Rosenthal, and Chris Shrodes, has been essential. Comments from Jeff Kipnis and Karen Soroca added much-needed focus to the text. Thanks are due to the participants of the 2001–2002 Baumer Seminars: Mitch Acock, Jin Choi, Steve Clark, Jeff Collins, Laurie Gunzelman, Tom Hanson, Brett Lewis, Sam Luckino, Stephanie Miller, Rujuta Mody, Chairman Mouse, Manoj Patel, Pavan Peter, Brian Reynolds, Angela Sutton, Tate Wilson, and Jie Zhu. Also, I thank Tracy Gannon, who took the time to travel with me to the Netherlands.

This book would not exist were it not for the efforts of Laurie Gunzelman, who organized the 2001–2002 Baumer Seminars and compiled much of the initial research, Mike Denison, who guided the project through to completion, and Teresa Ball. Lorraine Wild and Robert Ruehlman provided thoughtful design, and Kevin Lippert, Linda Lee, and Jennifer Thompson at Princeton Architectural Press offered essential direction and support. In addition, Acock Associates Architects and Atlas Blueprint and Supply both generously supported the project.

Finally, special thanks to Jeff Kipnis and Nicole Hill, for contributions too numerous to name.

ERASMUS BRIDGE Rotterdam, The Netherlands	Total Length: 802 m	Width of Shipping Passage below Cable-Stayed Bridge: 260 m
	Length of Cable-Stayed Bridge: 410 m	Top of Pylon: 139 m above sea level
	Length of Bascule Bridge: 89 m	Top of Bascule in Raised Position: 63 m above sea level

1986   1987   1988   1989   1990   1991

1986
Rotterdam Development Plan by Teun Koolhaas Associates suggests new bridge spanning the River Maas.

1987
Design work begins by Maarten Struijs, Public Works architect for the city of Rotterdam.

Ben van Berkel completes studies at the Architectural Association in London.

1988
Van Berkel and Bos Architectuurbureau established in Amsterdam.

December 1989
Program of requirements presented to the mayor and aldermen of Rotterdam.

Wim Quist and Ben van Berkel are brought on as aesthetic advisors to the design team by Professor Arie Krijgsman.

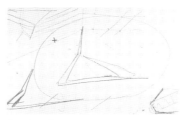

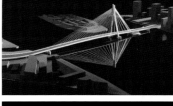

April 1990
Braced hockey stick and 4-pole designs are presented by the Public Works team.

May 1990
Maas Island plan presented.

September 1990
Ben van Berkel presents the bent-pylon scheme in reinforced concrete.

Width of Bascule Passage: 50 m	**Width of Traffic Deck on Cable-Stayed Bridge:** 33.8 m	**Width of Bicycle Paths:** 2 @ 2.6 m	**Total Weight of Cable-Stayed Bridge:** 6800 tons	**Total Length of Strands:** 515,100 m
Maximum Height of Traffic Deck: 17 m above sea level	**Width of Traffic Deck on Bascule Bridge:** 33.1 m	**Width of Automobile Lanes:** 2 @ 5.6 m	**Weight of Pylon:** 1800 tons	**Project Cost:** 365 million Dutch guilders (US$ 220 million)
Maximum Depth of Bridge Deck: 2.3 m	**Width of Footpaths:** 2 @ 2.45 m	**Width of Tramway:** 2 @ 3.15 m	**Weight of Stays:** 600 tons	**Traffic Capacity:** 26,000 vehicles per day
			Total Length of Stays: 6,180 m	

1992   1993   1994   1995   1996

1991
Steel arch plan presented by Lubbers and Weeber.

Virlogeux calculates concrete bent-pylon scheme and deems it unbuildable. Calls for steel pylon with backstays.

Fall 1991
Cost estimates are completed.

Bent-pylon scheme—365 million guilders.

4-pole scheme—325 million guilders.

14 November 1991
City council votes in favor of the bent-pylon scheme.

February 1992
Project is named Erasmus Bridge.

11 March 1995
Pylon is placed upright and welded to the rear spar.

13 April 1995
Pylon is floated to the site.

3 May 1995
Final Bridge section is put in place.

27 January 1996
Bascule ramp installed.

24 June 1996
Bascule is lowered, completing the bridge.

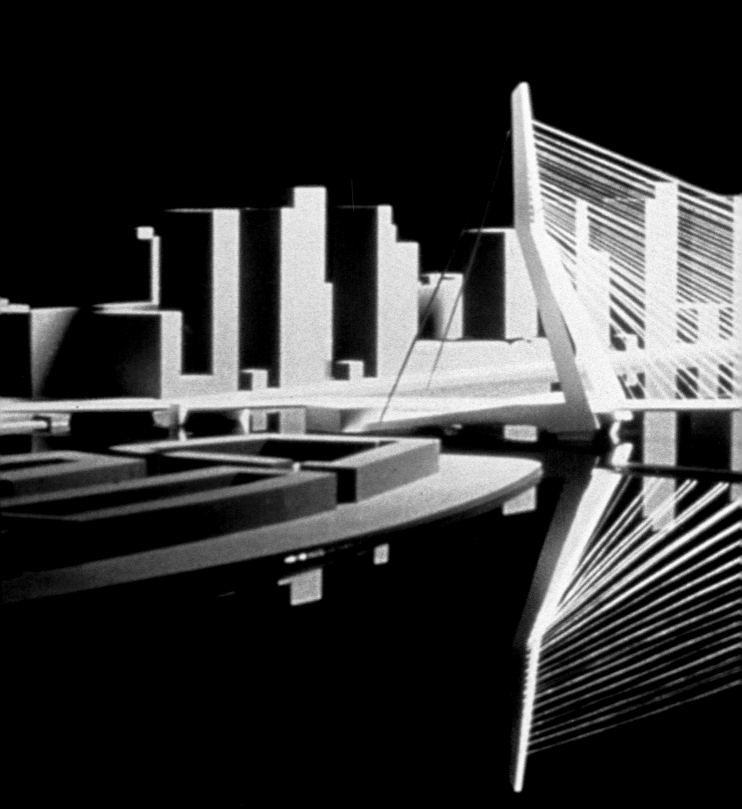

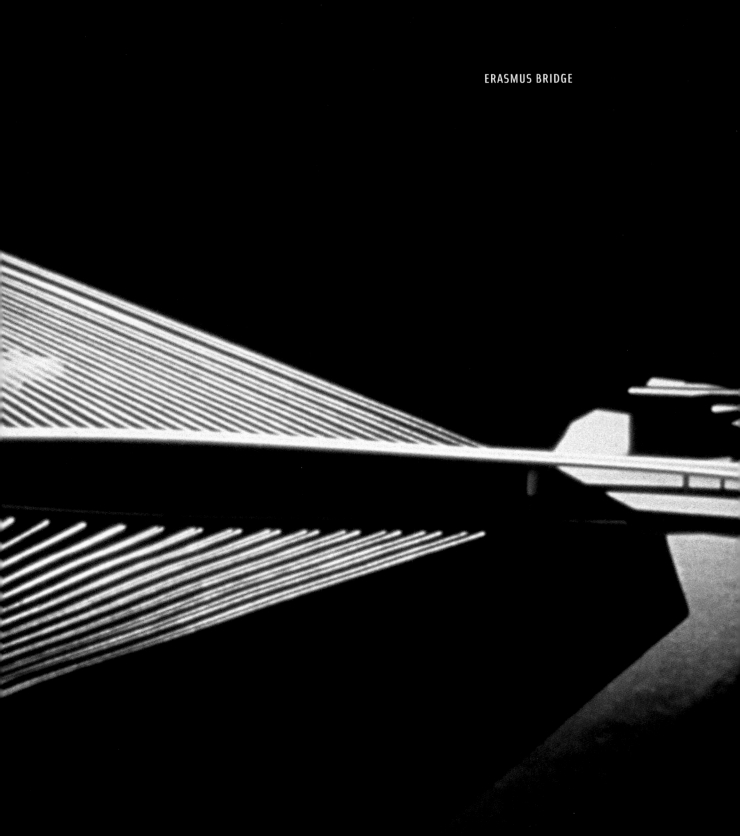

*The following was extracted from a series of interactions that took place
between Ben van Berkel, Caroline Bos, and the students and faculty of the
Knowlton School of Architecture during the 2001–2002 academic year.*

Ben van Berkel: For a long time, we were unhappy with the profession. It was unbelievable to us how boring architects were. We were not interested in working within the rigid hierarchies of traditional practice. We were looking for ways to expand our practice, to rethink the position of the architect. How could an architect operate in our culture? How could one be experimental?

We shared these attitudes with an incredible group of friends and colleagues, including Greg Lynn, Alejandro Zaera-Polo, and Jeff Kipnis, who continue to explore these issues with us. Each in their own way was interested in new techniques, new organizational possibilities, and new effects.

Through the 1990s, many practitioners were talking about the computer—about its potential for a radical reconfiguration of practice. At the same time, influenced by the writings of Deleuze and Guattari, we became interested in the topic of the diagram.

But for us, architecture had to be considered within the framework of the built environment— it could not operate solely within the realm of theory. We architects possess so much political responsibility. In many cases, we deal with larger sums of money than politicians do. Strangely, many architects react by pulling away from their role in the public realm, preferring to operate primarily in the arcane world of theory. Few would accuse architects of reticence, but in this case, perhaps, we do not communicate enough.

We wanted to open the lines of communication, to expand the discourse of the discipline beyond its insular boundaries and engage culture more directly. We wanted to look at contemporary techniques and explore how those techniques might work to redefine architectural practice. In doing so, perhaps we would discover the essence of architecture itself

Todd Gannon: What was it specifically about architectural practice that did not sit well with you?

BvB: Our concern had to do with the rigid, traditional hierarchies that organize the way we, as architects, have always worked. We were critical of the idea of the master builder. Was this concept a reasonable model for working? For with it came a very rigid, almost mechanical structure of lead architect, assistants, and draftspeople. We began our practice working with this model but found it too limiting. It was not conducive to experimentation.

In addition, we found too much of our time being consumed by those parts of the practice that had nothing to do with design. We would fight with the lawyers in the mornings and wrestle with the management and financial work in the evenings. This left little time for design itself.

We decided to transform ourselves into a much more experimental practice. We wanted to push the limits of architecture, to find new avenues to explore. We devoted ourselves to developing new design techniques in pursuit of new architectural effects.

Perhaps most importantly, we strove toward greater inclusiveness. This was the great lesson we learned working on the Erasmus Bridge. Here, we worked right alongside the engineers; we could not have done that project on our own. And with the computer, we were able to eliminate the traditional fragmentation of architectural practice.

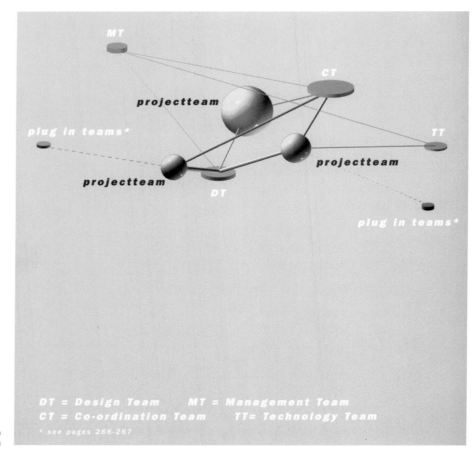

DT = Design Team   MT = Management Team
CT = Co-ordination Team   TT= Technology Team
* see pages 266-267

UN Studio
organizational diagram

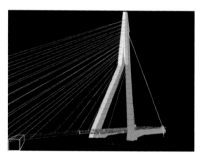

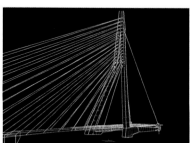

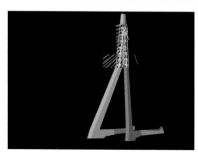

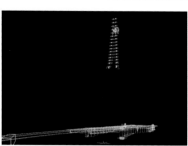

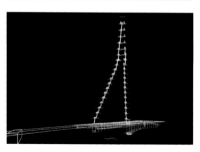

With the computer, we could see everything at once. Geometry, materials, structural forces, effects of light, paths of movement, and more were explored within the framework of that single machine. This sparked in us the idea to rethink everything in these new, inclusive terms.

But this was not simply a way to produce new forms; it became a way to explore new possibilities of organization. With these new tools, the old ways of working made no sense to us. Remember, architects first and foremost organize information, and the computer proved incredibly powerful at this task. It allowed us to be much more efficient, business-like, and clear. From this new organizational clarity, an enormous amount of freedom emerged—freedom for content.

TG: You and Caroline once wrote quite a bit of criticism. Could we think of criticism as another design tool, or does it serve a different purpose?

BvB: I believe that criticism is necessary. One must understand the culture in which one works, and writing provides a way to be imaginative about the work of one's colleagues. In that sense, it is certainly a tool.

I wish we had more time for it. Recently, we have been exploring possibilities in painting and sculpture through criticism. We have become infatuated with Georges Seurat. But we do not wish to enter the world of art criticism, we are simply exploring possibilities that might be exploited in architecture.

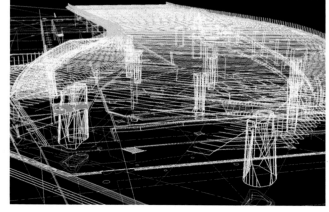

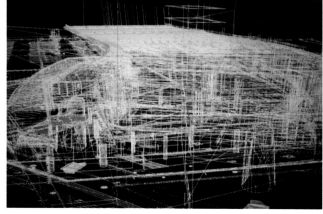

left: 3D models of the pylon

right, top and bottom:
Wire-frame models of
bridge deck

TG: Can you give us an example?

BvB: At the REMU electricity station in Amersfoort, the idea of using the basalt lava as a point of departure came from Joseph Beuys. Beuys worked with the material himself because he felt that it was related to the notion of frozen energy. At REMU, we became fascinated with the possibility that one could develop a project solely through an exploration of material effects. What could one do with a material? Could it construct an organization?

In the Erasmus Bridge, we derived the concrete piers from an interest in the sculpture of Constantin Brancusi. As I've said many times, we really considered the piers to be more important than the bridge itself.

We are fascinated in the possibilities of anything to be translated into architecture. We try to be as open as possible, to the point of being absurd. If you establish effective translation techniques, you can translate anything. To do this effectively, you need an instrument, akin to a kaleidoscope, that will twist the thing beyond recognition. This is the place where real discoveries are made.

The diagram is exactly this kind of machine; through it you can tune the idea, make subtle modulations and manipulations. I could do an entire book on the diagram—there are so many types to be analyzed. With the Brancusi reference, we are dealing with an image diagram. The operation is one of turning an image into an organization.

REMU Electricity Substation, Amersfoort, The Netherlands, 1989–94

TG: This is the crucial step—the translation. Often we see in student work a tendency to do very intelligent research and interesting diagrams, then simply blow them up to the scale of a building. The lack of translation is frustrating.

BvB: Yes, one has to learn to let go of the diagram. It is about developing a means of instrumentalizing the process. It is not about developing a diagram that makes an interesting form, but about learning from it its organizational principles, from how it works.

In the end, you have to invent your own tools. I am not the first one to talk about the diagram. It is a very personal investigative tool. You must have your own agenda. In order to be an architect, you must project your own beliefs into the project.

This is why we are so interested in painting, or, more specifically, in the obsessions of painters. It is rare to find an architect who can throw himself into his work the way a painter does. Many architects don't know how to engage their own work. Think of the incredibly subtle refinements of a painter like Seurat or Vermeer. These artists developed a very personal set of techniques and secrets. They developed a kind of cookbook to making the work.

TG: That is a funny analogy. Because in architecture, there is a long history of cookbooks intended to be used by anyone—from Vitruvius to Alberti, Durand to Le Corbusier. But if we look at the results, we see that the best work came from the most personalized practices, those architects who figured out how to twist the rules to their own ends.

BvB: You are right; one has to be in the work. Dogmatic rules will not produce the results you want.

top: Joseph Beuys, *7000 Oaks*,
Kassel, Switzerland, 1982,
basalt lava steles and oak tree

bottom, left: Georges Seurat,
The Bridge at Courbevoie,
1886–87

bottom, right: Jan Vermeer,
The Art of Painting, 1666–73

I have become interested in the medium of photography in recent years. I've been using our built work as a subject, but it is not a process of mere documentation. They are in a very real sense a continuation of the design work, a sort of finishing touch. Tools like Photoshop allow me to make subtle improvements to the work, or in some cases, radical transformations. I think of it as painting with the camera. We are attempting to get beyond the fragmentary representation of artifacts to a presentation of the essence of each project—that essence transformed through the medium of the photograph.

The method allows us to experiment with the proportioning of information. Many of these pieces, such as the Erasmus Bridge photo, have a long history of their own. For almost ten years I have been tinkering with the image, refining it, searching for all the things it can tell me.

All of these methods, whether it is writing, photography, or architectural design, represent incredible struggles for both myself and Caroline. But this struggle is important. Even collaboration is a struggle. I still find it difficult to work with a lot of people, which is always the case when working on architecture.

Writing is the opposite; it is an isolated process. You can get criticism and advice from friends and colleagues, but often that leads the piece in a direction you were not headed in the first place. It is important to maintain a balance, so, for us, writing and architecture have to support each other. Each represents a form of language, forms that possess their own rules and their own limitations.

above:
Constantin Brancusi,
Golden Bird, c. 1916

left: Ben van Berkel,
When the Cathedrals are Blue, 1999,
photographic print on polyester cloth

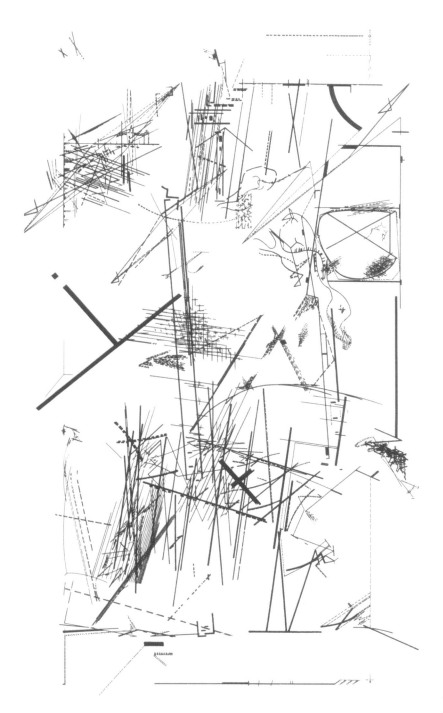

Daniel Libeskind,
Chamber Works, 1983

TG: Think of a practitioner with ambitions similar to your own but setting out into the field twenty years earlier. The 1970s and 1980s were a tough time for building. There were very few commissions, even fewer for young practitioners with progressive ideas and little experience. As a result, many important architects retreated from traditional practice into the more arcane world of architectural theory. Think of the incredibly singular explorations that began the careers of Steven Holl or Bernard Tschumi or Daniel Libeskind—each alone in a studio in New York laboring away on these incredible drawing projects.

At the same point in your career you found yourself embroiled in building the Erasmus Bridge. In your case, there was simply no time for sustained contemplation. You had no choice but to embrace the realities of construction, of management, of budgets.

This marks a radical difference from the previous generation. In the 1970s there were no jobs, no money, no possibility for projects for so many architects. It was only natural to develop an academic position. But in the booming economy of the 1990s, one found practitioners who, whether through competitions or connections or blind luck, found themselves in positions where they had no choice but to dive in headfirst.

Yours was not a problem of how to react against the establishment, of how to be subversive, but a much more difficult task of how to develop a position within the contingencies of a highly complex and very real civic project. In contrast to those architects who spent extended periods of time working out their theoretical ambitions on imagined projects with imagined constraints, you found yourself having to develop a way of working that embraced exactly those traditional structures that so many others set out to criticize.

I would argue that these conditions had as much to do with this reconfiguration of practice you discuss as anything else. Would you agree?

BvB: That is a beautiful explanation of how it came together. It was a kind of implosion of all that we wanted to do in architecture but could not prove. We discovered that one does not have to think through theory in order to make form, the process did not have to be sequential. It was possible to build theoretical ideas alongside the development of the physical artifact.

It was here that we developed our philosophy of the diagram. The Erasmus Bridge was the ultimate diagram process. There was no preconceived theory we wanted to work with; we had no a priori system in place. Instead, we embraced a staccato of moments in which several diagrams came together and transformed into the operational principles for the structure of the bridge. Conceptual and material concerns came together simultaneously. The bridge became both our manifesto and its proof.

TG: The bridge was not the only project you were working on at the time. How did this new manner of thinking effect concurrent projects?

BvB: The bridge project developed very slowly. It first appeared in 1991 but did not turn into a real project for the office until 1992 or 1993. At that time we were also involved in two small projects in Amersfoort, the Karbouw office building and the REMU electricity substation.

The REMU project was an opportunity to refine our skills with the computer. We used a matrix of three-dimensional coordinates to determine the curved surfaces of the project. Early design studies developed and became the method by which the actual stone blocks were manufactured. We crafted the forms as well as the effects digitally.

We were interested in exploring the nature of the detail. What new possibilities did they harbor? Corporal compactness, an idea we outlined in our book *Mobile Forces*, was explored specifically in the substation. The building was to be understood as a body—it could not be read as a simple surface. We were interested in making a strong statement without resorting to a box or some other strong geometrical form. We were much more interested in the possibilities of the material and the detail.

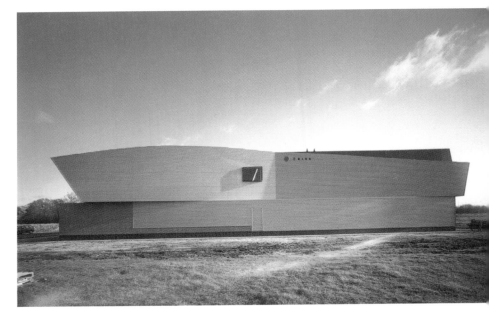

Karbouw offices and workshop,
Amersfoort, The Netherlands, 1990–92

above and right: REMU,
1989–94
exterior details

Erasmus Bridge Rotterdam 1990-96

The scandal-filled life of the Erasmus Bridge has turned it into a typical late-twentieth century media star. Adoration, public humiliation, health problems, a spell in rehabilitation; the bridge has seen it all. Does it hurt to see architecture dragged down to this level? Or is it better that architecture be part of mass culture rather than stay in its ivory tower? Shouldn't architecture engage people?

Baby-blue monster

'Mobile Forces' was the accompanying battle cry, as the Erasmus Bridge was meant from its earliest, most sketchy beginnings to incorporate the multitude of changeable public, urban, economic, political and constructive considerations that direct all large-scale projects.

The bridge is the product of an integrated design approach. Construction, urbanism, infrastructure and public functions are given shape in one comprehensive gesture. To achieve fluent working relationships between the different parties involved, the whole design and building process took place in Auto-Cad, enhancing control on all levels and significantly deepening the insight of the architect in the technical design. During preliminary and definitive design phases, the design was continuously refined. The five differently

TG: How did these ideas translate into the Erasmus Bridge project?

Caroline Bos: The Erasmus Bridge was a formative project in the thinking of UN Studio. We had only been in practice for about two years when the project came our way, and its complexity and scope required us to unlearn all of our training and leave behind our preconceived notions of architecture.

The introductory text we wrote in our book, *Move*, outlined the early life of the Erasmus Bridge. Just one month after its opening by the Queen in 1996, the cables started to move violently due to rain and wind-induced vibrations. It eventually turned out to be a small technical problem, easily solved by modifying the position of the shock absorbers, but in the public eye, this was a major scandal. For this reason, there has never been a publication on the bridge.

That scandal has for the most part died down and the bridge has been featured in numerous Dutch advertising and political campaigns, especially those that wished to profess their innovation and daring. Yet the hint of that scandal remains. Perhaps any project must go through that sort of thing to achieve success.

Excerpt from Ben van Berkel and Caroline Bos, *Move*, 1999

shaped concrete piers, the railings, the landings, the details of fixtures and joints and the maintenance equipment were all integrally designed.
Rising to a height of 139 metres and spanning a width of 800 metres, the bridge over the river Maas forms an orientation point within the city. The asymmetric pylon with its bracket construction in sky-coloured steel has 2000 different facades. The long, diagonal cables physically and metaphorically link Rotterdam South to the City Centre. Thirty-two stays attached to the top of the pylon and eight backstays keep the construction in balance. Five concrete piers carry the steel deck that is divided into different traffic lanes: two footpaths, two cycle tracks, tram rails and two carriageways for cars.
Sweeping concrete staircases lead up from the parking garage on the north side, extending the curve of the landing to pedestrian level and contributing to the public quality of the bridge as a square in the sky.
At night, when the bridge is reduced to a silhouette, a special light project emphasises the interior of the bridge, with its bundled cables rising high above the water as a dematerialised reflection of its daytime identity.

The bridge was just one component in a larger redevelopment project spearheaded by Riek Bakker, the public works director for Rotterdam. The city had developed extensively to the west of the bridge site, leaving the immediate area, known as Kop van Zuid, desolate. Bakker's concept was to develop a dense urban intervention on the southern shore of the River Maas, what she called "Manhattan on the Maas." In 1986, she commissioned Teun Koolhaas Associates to devise a master plan.

In addition to a series of high-rise buildings on the southern shore, Koolhaas's plan proposed a new connection between the historic center to the north and the new developments to the south. This would, of course, become the Erasmus Bridge. From the beginning, this bridge was to be more than a simple connection. It was intended to have an iconic status, to act as an attractor for new development to the riverfront. The city felt that in order to entice development, they had to lead the way.

BvB: The city architect had been working on the project for three years before we were invited to consult. Our role was strange: We were not to design anything, we were there simply to comment on the design work of the city architect. The unspoken fact was that we were hired to kill the project. The city aldermen said to us, "Whatever you do, find a way to prove that this bridge could be more than a simple connector, that it can somehow be related to the history and future of Rotterdam."

CB: We felt the bridge should derive from the distinct character of Rotterdam. Rotterdam has always had an industrial character, quite different from the administrative formality of the Hague or the picturesque quality of Amsterdam. Rotterdam is by far the most modern of the three cities, owing largely to the fact that it was horribly bombed during the Second World War.

Rotterdam, view of the River Maas

Teun Koolhaas, aerial view of
Rotterdam master plan, 1986

top: Swing bridge over the Koningshaven, 1876

middle: Fixed arch bridge over the Maas, 1877

bottom: The "Hef" lift bridge, 1926

top: Koninginne swing bridge, 1876

middle: The old Willems bridge, 1878–1981

bottom: The Koninginne bascule bridge, 1929

Rotterdam's bridges reveal its industrial past. The first to cross the Maas appeared in the late nineteenth century, a product of the expansion of the Dutch railway system. The earliest are gone, but a very important early bridge, known as the Hef, remains. After the construction of a railway tunnel, the bridge was no longer needed, but the proposal for its demolition was met with such strong protest that the Hef remains to this day.

Bridge building in Rotterdam tends to coincide with major developments. The city underwent a major postwar building boom, and, by the 1960s, traffic had become unbearable. A new ring road was constructed, requiring a tunnel and a new bridge, the van Brienenoord, in 1965. Traffic has steadily increased since, compelling the construction of the second van Brienenoord bridge, an identical twin to the first, in 1990.

The last bridge built in central Rotterdam before the Erasmus Bridge was the new Willems bridge, a cable-stayed bridge with two pylons completed by the public works architect Maarten Struijs in 1981. With its bright red color, it quickly became a cherished landmark in the city. When the project for the Erasmus Bridge began, the team responsible for the Willems Bridge was reassembled.

top left: The van Brienenoord bridge, 1965

top right: The second van Brienenoord bridge, 1990

bottom: The new Willems bridge, 1981

Struijs and his team prepared a series of bridge designs beginning with a four-pole design similar in concept to the Willems Bridge. Bakker felt that this scheme lacked a strong urban presence, so additional proposals were made. As the project progressed, new members were added to the team. For us, perhaps the most important was an engineer from Delft, Professor Arie Krijgsman. Krijgsman quickly invited two others to consult on the project, Wim Quist, an established Dutch architect, and Ben van Berkel, who was completely unknown at the time.

TG: What was the relationship with Krijgsman? Why did he choose Ben for the project?

CB: They met while Ben was a visiting critic at the University of Delft. This was 1989; our office had existed for barely a year. We had completed a few small projects but were mainly known through our writing.

In fact, Bakker had commissioned us a year earlier to compose a study of all the development projects that had been proposed for the area. Our report was very critical—it actually made us a few enemies in Rotterdam even before we were considered to work on the bridge. I think some of those hard feelings remain, since we have not gotten a single project in Rotterdam since.

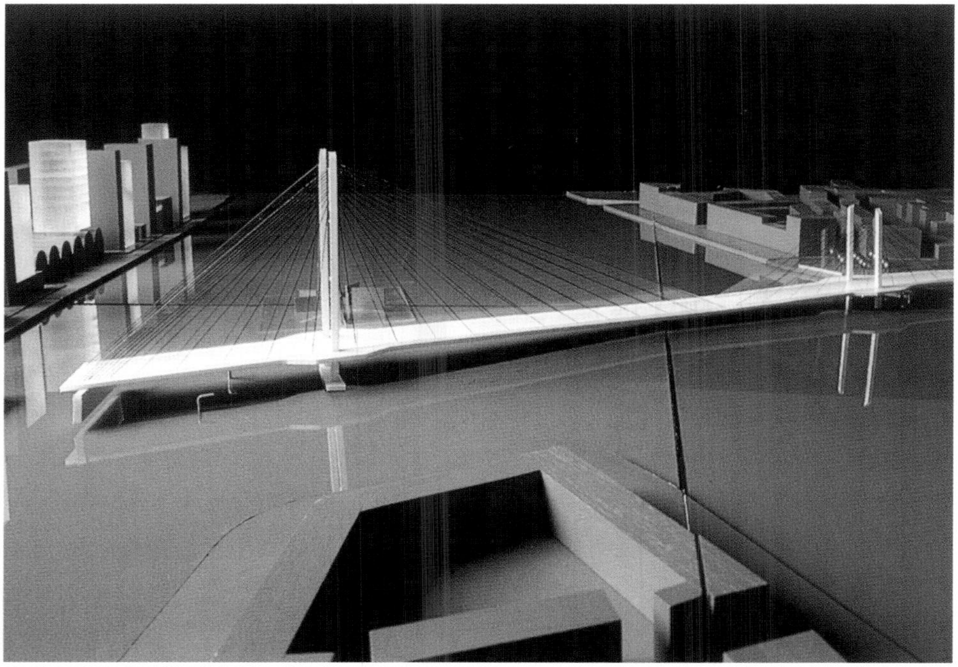

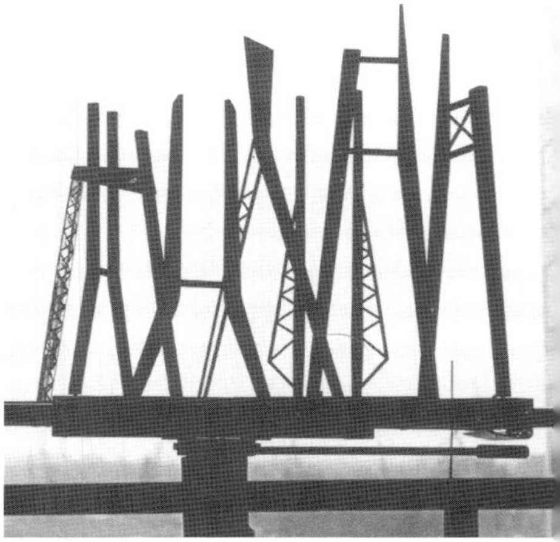

above: Maarten Struijs, pylon studies

opposite: Braced hockey-stick scheme

Four-pole scheme, model

I still find it hard to believe that we were chosen at all. Bakker strongly disagreed with our analysis, but she was willing to trust that we were a competent architectural firm.

TG: After the four-pole scheme, the next major iteration was the so-called "braced hockey stick." This proposal, with its single pylon and bent mast configuration, heads in the direction of the realized design. Was this a result of the criticism of Ben and Wim Quist?

CB: Indirectly. The design process was long and very complicated. At the beginning, Ben and Quist were not allowed to draw anything—their role was solely to provide commentary and criticism. But this could not last. Very soon, Quist said that he could not be involved without drawing. They had both been secretly sketching already, who could resist? It was just a matter of time before their ideas made their way into the formal discussions about the project.

Soon afterward, Ben produced a sketch in which he conceived of the pylon as this inverted hook, very similar to the final scheme. Everyone involved became interested, except perhaps for Struijs, and Ben's single-pylon design was developed.

In the meantime, Struijs came up with the "braced hockey stick." From here, the process started to get pretty messy. The newspapers were getting involved; there were leaks to the press . . .

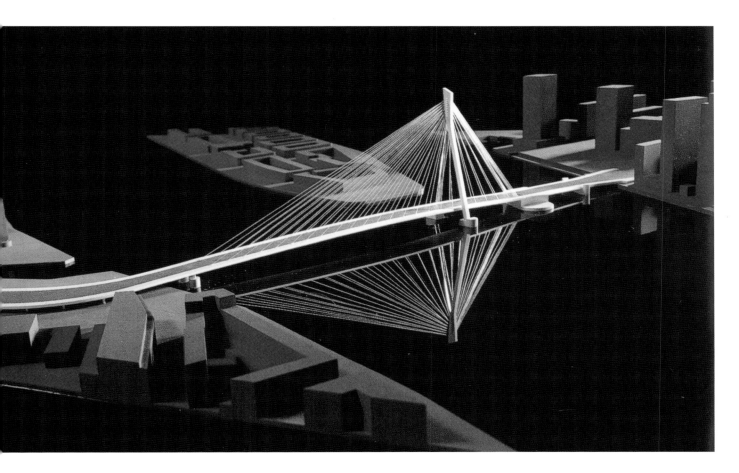

top and bottom:
Ben van Berkel,
single-pylon sketches

To complicate matters, another architect, Carel Weeber, proposed a third scheme, a steel-arch design. His thinking was that if two dogs are fighting for a bone, a third could run off with it. But the arch scheme was eventually rejected, as was the Maas Island Plan by Rob Lubbers, which proposed two bridges and an artificial island with shops, restaurants, and so forth off the tip of Noordereiland.

TG: There was some resistance from the citizens of Rotterdam as well. A vocal group was against the idea of any bridge at the site.

CB: Yes, there were concerns over the need for a bridge at all, as well as for the costs involved. A project of this magnitude cannot help but generate some inconve-

nience. In this case, some residents of the Noordereiland became very vocal. But the city has quite a bit of experience handling large-scale infrastructural works, and with the help of various public advisory committees the problems were minimized.

The greater difficulty was financial. The four-pole design had been estimated at 325 million guilders, and our proposal was 365 million. In the end, the entire process came down to a city council vote. In an unbelievably unDutch turn of events, our project was chosen.

While the presentations and deliberations were going on, a bomb threat forced the evacuation of the town hall. It turned out to be just a hoax, but it was indicative of just how tense the situation had become.

Carel Weeber, steel-arch scheme

And this was just the beginning. The real challenge began with the actual design and construction of this bridge. The project was still to be officially handled by the city engineering department of Rotterdam. Struijs had had their support throughout the preliminary process, and now we all had to put everything behind us and work together.

We were never awarded a full contract for the bridge. We had to negotiate every year to remain on the project. Many of them seemed to think they could just congratulate us, brush us aside, and move on with the project. But we were determined to have a lead role in the construction documentation. The detailing of the project was critical to us; we were not about to turn it over to the engineers.

It has become increasingly common practice in architecture to separate the roles of the design architect from those who make the construction documents. We continue to resist this trend. For us, it is the material condition of the finished work that matters most.

If a great idea is poorly executed, in the end you have a poor project.

We set up an office in Rotterdam in the same building as the city engineers. They devoted two departments to work on the bridge. Two hundred people for the steel and two hundred for the concrete. We worked hard to develop a close relationship with the project team, and we stayed in constant contact with the politicians, endlessly reinforcing the idea that it was the detailing that would make or break the project.

TG: The whole thing sounds rather like a fairy tale. A thirty-year-old architect with no experience comes out of nowhere and steals the biggest project in the country.

CB: I think it was a total fluke. Luck has a lot to do with something like that, you can never plan for it. But once we got the chance, we were not going to lose it. A chance like that, so early in one's career and not won by competition, is an incredible opportunity.

TG: How did the design of the bridge develop?

BvB: We began by thinking about how the bridge could be more than a simple connection between the old center to the north and the new development to the south. We felt that the bridge should evoke Rotterdam's industrial aura without directly mimicking it. We wanted something subtler, for the bridge to take on and project the optimistic political tone of Rotterdam. The bridge is not directly referential—it would be impossible to draw it back to a single precedent. But its form nonetheless refers to the shipyards, the cranes, and the industrial character of the Rotterdam harbor.

Of course, I could not help but draw upon my experience working in the office of Santiago Calatrava. I was very impressed with the way he worked. He was incredibly quick in how he analyzed forces in a structure. I tried to emulate that quickness by working in very close contact with the city engineers.

I maintain a high regard for Calatrava, but I am critical of certain aspects of his work. While each of his bridges is undeniably impressive in terms of its structural innovation and imagery, I think they are less successful as urban interventions. They exist as discreet objects, conceptually removed from the life of the city. I was always more interested in how a project could insinuate itself deeply into the fabric of the city. This became a primary concern for us in Rotterdam. The paths for different kinds of movement—pedestrians, bicycles, cars, and trams—branch out from the structure of the bridge and weave into the city fabric.

CB: A series of simple diagrams outlined our ideas about the site. From the beginning, we held a desire to maintain the feeling of the riverfront. The Maas is very wide to the north of Noordereiland, and we were determined to keep the views open from the north shore and to maintain the continuity of the river. We accomplished this by placing the pylon on axis with the island. The pylon acts as a mediator between the two halves of the city as well as a discreet symbol for the city as a whole.

Site diagrams

Experience from Coolsingel

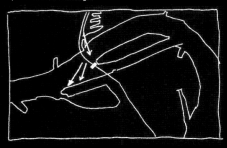

2 Pylon as Mediator

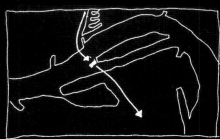

3 River Experience

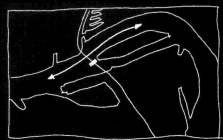

4 Relation between Bridges

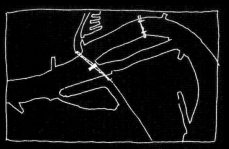

5 Symbolic Function for the Two Parts of the City

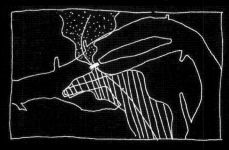

6 Opening the River Maas

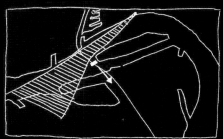

7 Visual Reference Point

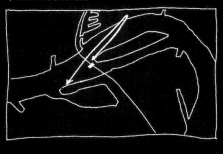

8 Image of Rotterdam

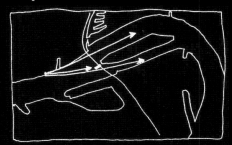

9 Composition

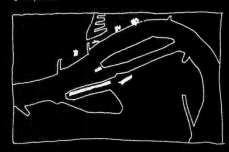

10 Entrance to Rotterdam

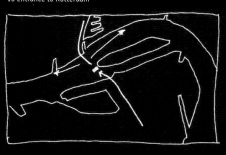

BvB: Early schemes by the city architect were very tall, some over 150 meters. The city planners felt that a bridge of that height overpower the proposed development beyond, so they asked for a shorter proposal. Our first investigations were simply about how to solve the height problem in a single pylon design. As we analyzed the forces at play, we saw that a straight pylon with uniformly distributed stay cables has the greatest bending moment at the middle; it wants to bend toward the cables. We discovered that if you bend the pylon in the other direction, the loads are decreased. The result is a dynamic resistance—it acts like a taut compound bow.

We illustrated the structural idea with a simple photograph. The ruler shows that when compressive forces are applied to a vertical element, a bend comes naturally. The idea was more explicitly outlined in a series of moment diagrams. The bent pylon produces more complex forces with smaller loads than the simple moment of the straight pylon. This gave us a shorter pylon that took less material to build, resulting in a more economical construction.

In addition, we achieved an entirely different proportion between the span of the bridge and the height of the pylon. In Calatrava's bridge in Seville, the relation is one to one—the bridge is as tall as its span. In Rotterdam, we were able to span 284 meters with a 139-meter pylon. It is, we feel, a more elegant solution.

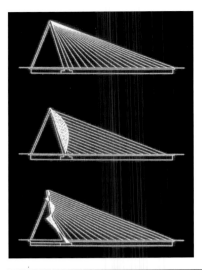

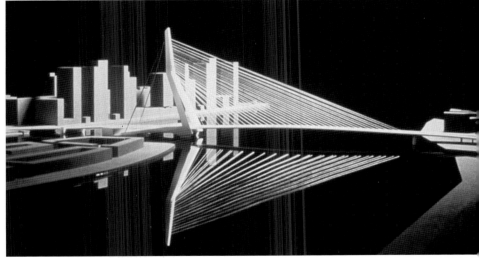

top, left: Pylon force diagrams

top, right: Illustration of the "taut bow" concept using a ruler

bottom: Erasmus Bridge, model

opposite, top: Ben van Berkel, Erasmus Bridge, view from west

opposite, bottom: Santiago Calatrava, Alamillo Bridge, Seville, Spain, 1987–92

Pylon, south elevation

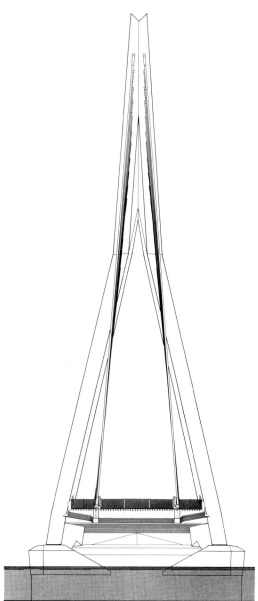

Pylon, north elevation

40 PYLON

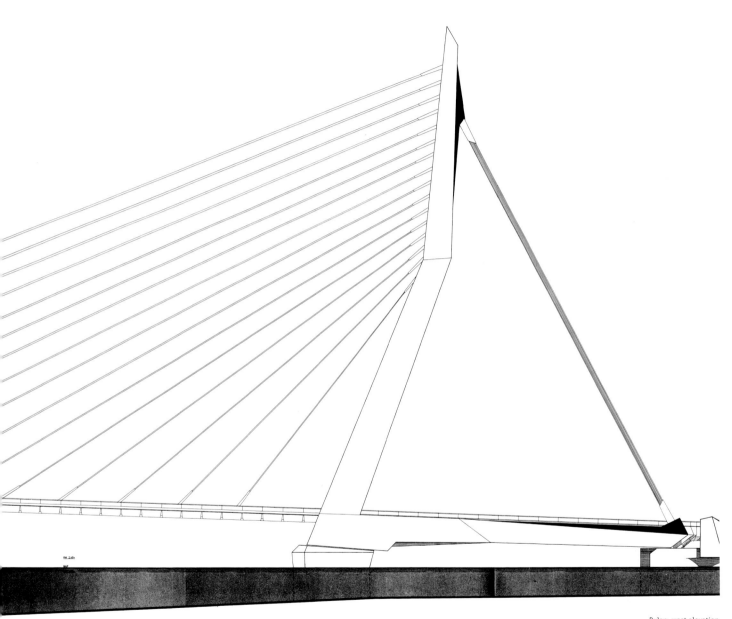

Pylon, west elevation

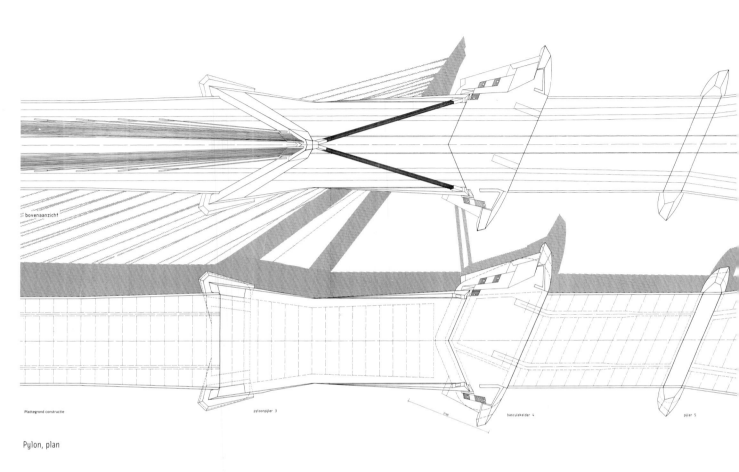

bovenaanzicht

Plattegrond constructie   pyloonpijler 3   star   basculekelder 4   pijler 5

Pylon, plan

"The shape of the pylon is very interesting, especially because whatever is not quite natural
 is a challenge nonetheless. If this bridge had been designed by a structural engineer,
 it would never have had such a powerful form because the form would then have been based
 on forces and moments." M. Kuijpers, *Project and Site Manager, Steel cable-stayed bridge,*
Rotterdam Public Works Department

A shorter pylon must resist a heavier dead load than more conventional single-pylon designs. Our original intent was to construct the pylon out of concrete with low backstays (see sketch, p.30), to let the sheer mass of the structure resist the forces.

But steel construction brought with it incredible advantages. By building in steel, it was possible to construct the superstructure indoors in a remote location, saving significant time and money and also giving us higher quality workmanship. The pylon was fabricated in

Vlissingen and floated to the site in one piece. An offshore construction company, Heerema, built the pylon. Their specialty is heavy construction on the open sea—oil rigs and such; they had no experience with a project like this. What they had, however, was huge amounts of warehouse space and an enormous crane. That crane made them the only contractor capable of bringing the pylon to the site in one piece, and with that they were able to tender a bid twenty million guilders lower than the next contractor.

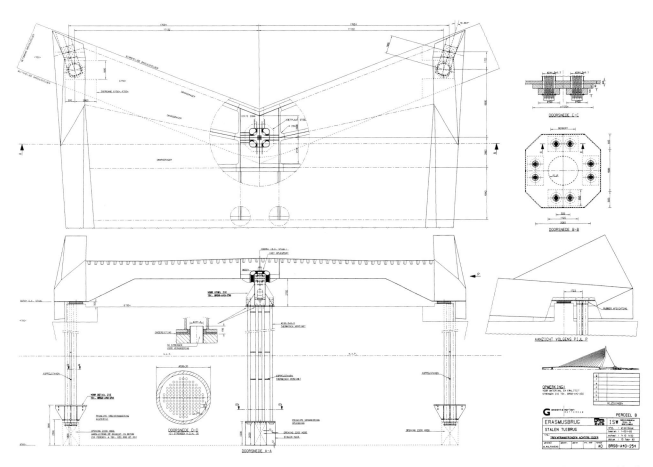

Pylon heel, plan, section, and details

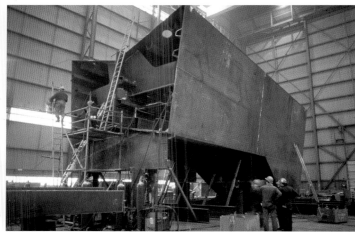

Off-site fabrication

Heerema had another secret weapon as well. They were able to perform all cutting and milling directly from our AutoCAD files using CAD-CAM technology. The process was simple: our office determined the critical points in a 3-D model. We then transferred these files directly to the engineers, who ran the structural calculations, and then passed the information to the contractor, who fabricated each piece. While this seamless interface is common practice today, in 1992 it was revolutionary.

The pylon is actually composed of three sections: the vertical, wishbone-shaped element and two horizontal "heels" that run along the edge of the bridge. Building off site, both the heel sections and the pylon itself could be constructed horizontally, allowing access to the entire height of the structure with an existing indoor gantry crane.

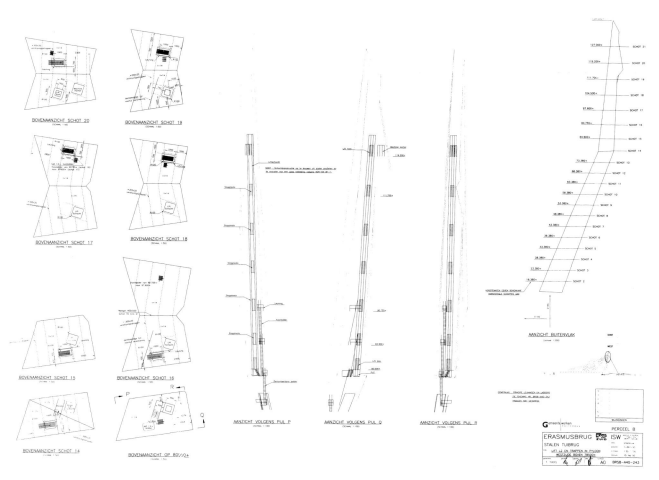

Pylon, horizontal and vertical sections

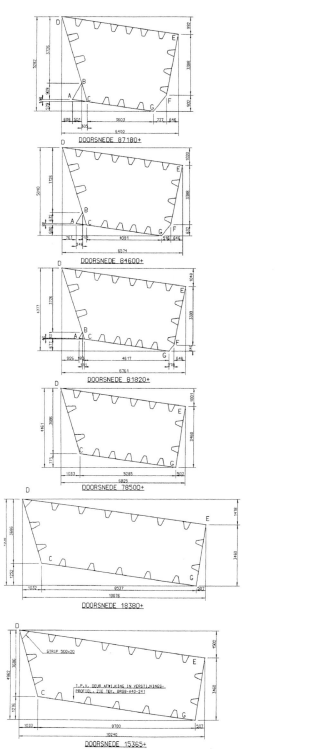

DOORSNEDE 87180+

DOORSNEDE 84600+

DOORSNEDE 81820+

DOORSNEDE 78500+

DOORSNEDE 18380+

STRIP 500x20

T.P.V. DEUR AFWIJKING IN VERSTIJVINGS-
PROFIEL, ZIE TEK. BRSB-A40-241

DOORSNEDE 15365+

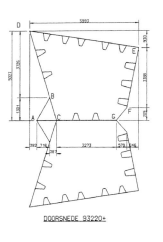

DOORSNEDE 93220+

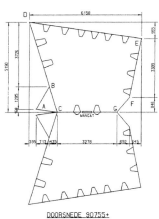

MANGAT

DOORSNEDE 90755+

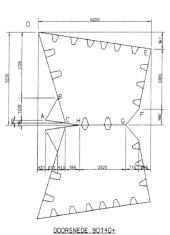

MANGAT

DOORSNEDE 90140+

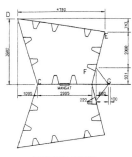

MANGAT

DOORSNEDE 113560+

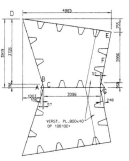

VERST. PL.800x40
OP 108100+

DOORSNEDE 109980+

MANGAT

DOORSNEDE 106470+

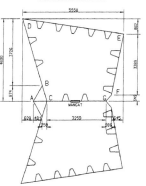

MANGAT

DOORSNEDE 99680+

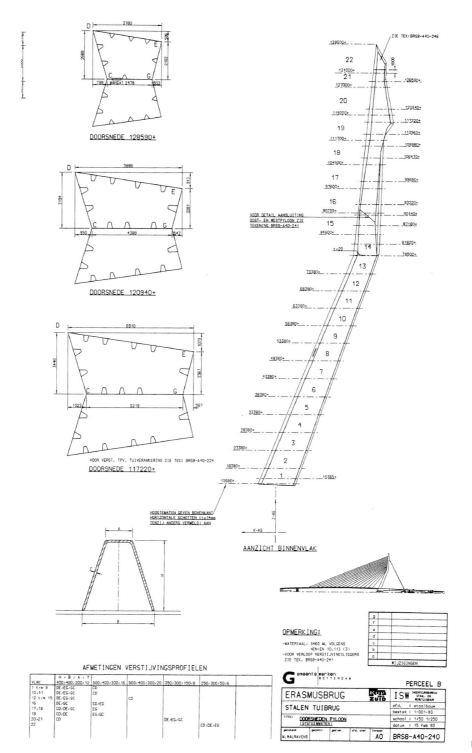

DOORSNEDE 128590+

DOORSNEDE 120940+

VOOR VERST. TPV. TUIVERANKERING ZIE TEK: BRS8-A40-224

DOORSNEDE 117220+

ZIE TEK: BRS8-A40-246

VOOR DETAIL AANSLUITING
OOST- EN WESTPYLOON ZIE
TEKENING BRS8-A40-241

HOOGTEMATEN GEVEN BOVENKANT
HORIZONTALE SCHOTTEN (t=14mm
TENZIJ ANDERS VERMELD) AAN

X-AS

AANZICHT BINNENVLAK

AFMETINGEN VERSTIJVINGSPROFIELEN

VLAK	H / B / A / t 400/400/200/12	500/400/300/16	500/400/300/20	350/300/150/8	250/300/50/6
1 t/m 9	DE/EG/GC	CD			
10-11	DE/EG/GC	CD			
12 t/m 15	DE/EG/GC		CD		
16	DE/GC			CD/EG	
17-18	CD/EG/GC			EG	
19	CD/DE			EG/GC	
20-21	CD			DE/EG/GC	
22					CD/DE/EG

OPMERKING:

-MATERIAAL: S460 ML VOLGENS
 NEN-EN 10.113 (3)
-VOOR VERLOOP VERSTIJVINGSLIGGERS
 ZIE TEK. BRS8-A40-243

g	
f	
e	
d	
c	
b	
a	
	WIJZIGINGEN

Gemeente werken
ROTTERDAM

PERCEEL B

ERASMUSBRUG   Kop
STALEN TUIBRUG   Zuid   ISW INGENIEURSBUREAU
                                STAAL- EN
                                WERKTUIGBOUW

TITEL: DOORSNEDEN PYLOON
       (SYSTEEMMATEN)

ofd. : staalbouw
bestek : 1-001-93
schaal : 1:50 1:250
datum : 15 feb 93

getekend: W. WALRAVENS | gecontr. | gezien | afd. chef | formaat: A0 | BRS8-A40-240

Pylon, sections

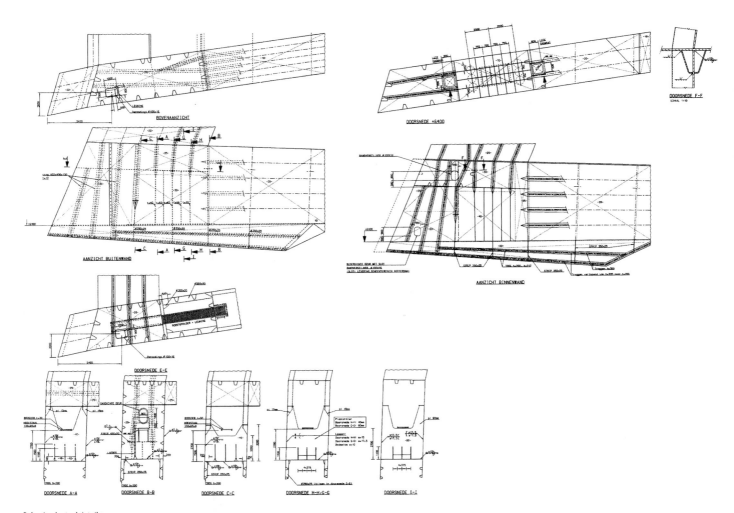

Pylon heel, steel details

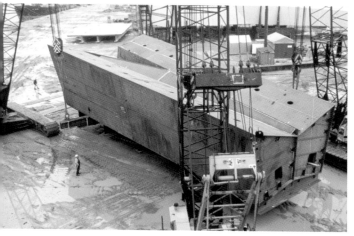

on assembly

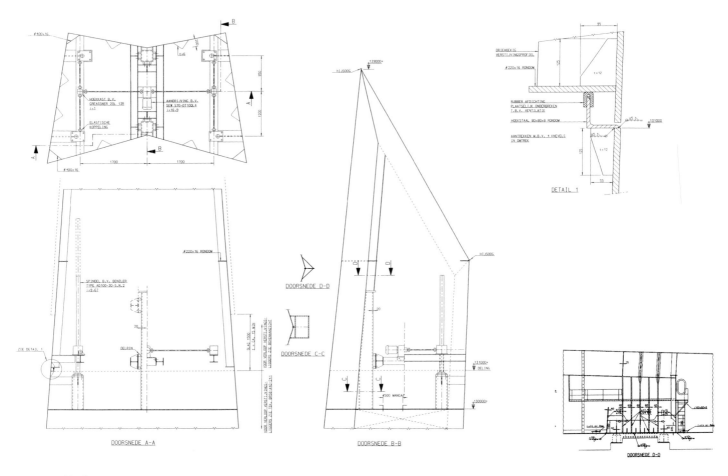

DOORSNEDE A-A

DOORSNEDE B-B

DOORSNEDE C-C

DOORSNEDE D-D

DETAIL 1

Pylon top, steel details

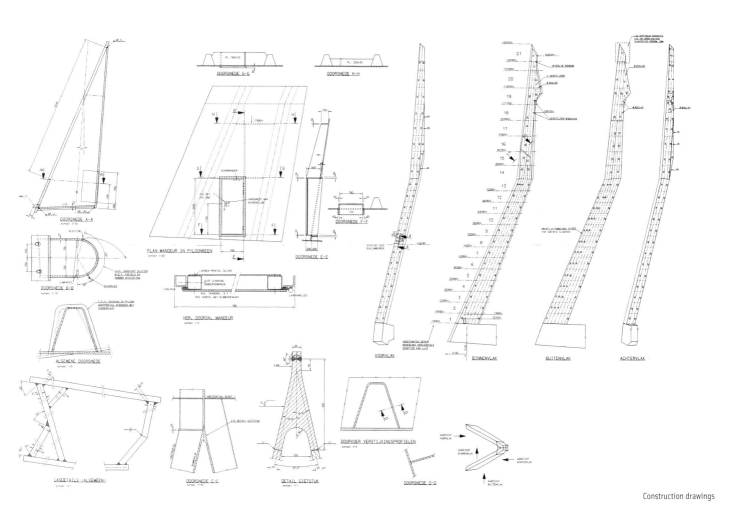

Construction drawings

"What made this special for us was not the quantity of steel or the scale of the project. It was more what you don't see: the complexity of the structure. With the Erasmus Bridge we were constructing a form that had to be fine and elegant; the forces were all absorbed by an invisible structure inside the pylon." P. Heerema, *Managing Director, Heerema Fabrication Group*

Transportation of the pylon
to Rotterdam via barge

With the three sections complete, the heels were placed on a barge offshore, and this huge, floating crane, two hundred meters tall, placed the pylon on the heels, where the entire assembly was welded together. A large steel frame provided temporary support until a sufficient number of stay cables were put in place.

The completed assembly was then floated down the Maas to the bridge site. During high tide, the pylon was positioned over the foundation. The pontoon it rested on was then flooded, and the pylon lowered into place.

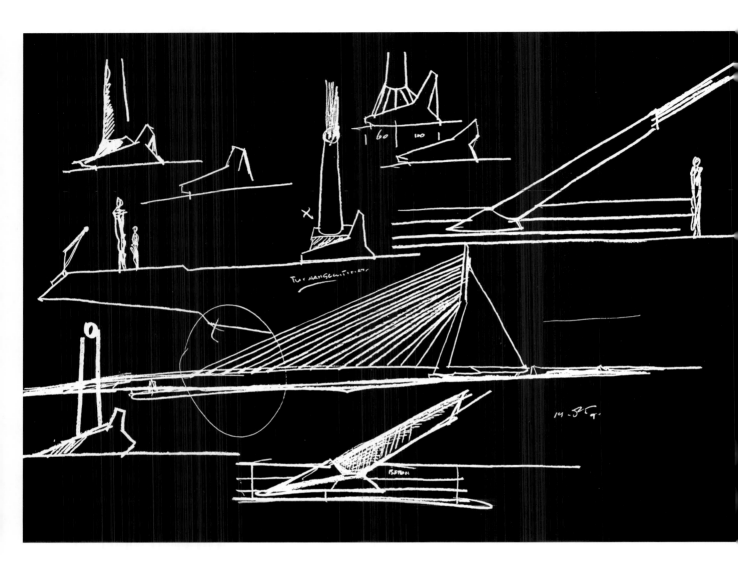

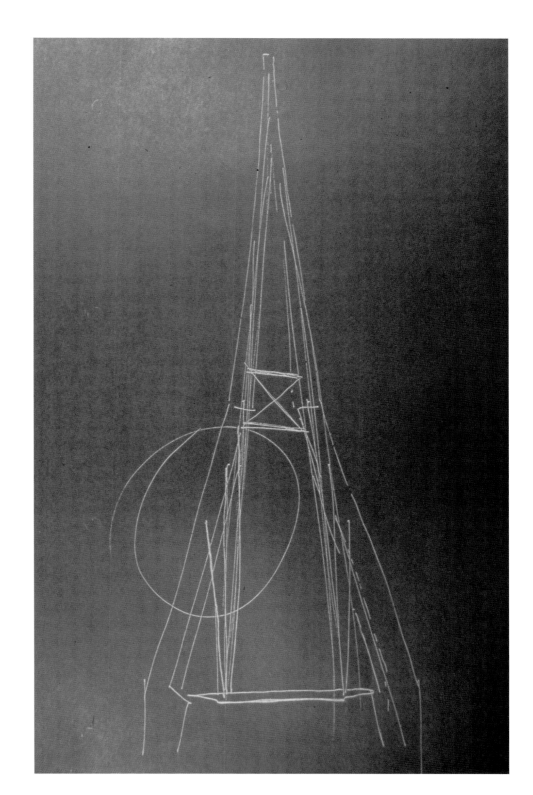

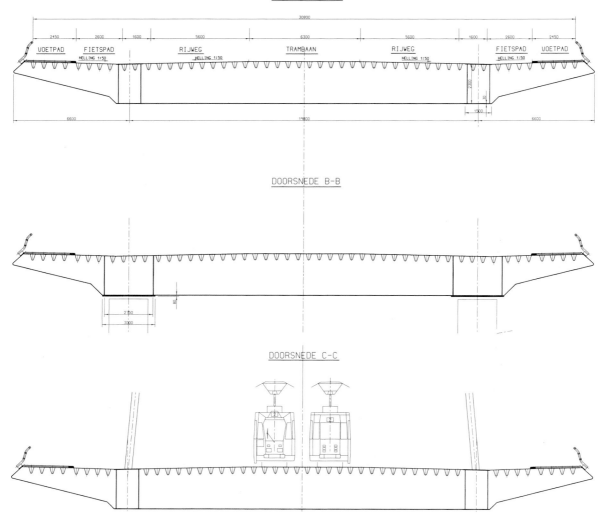

DOORSNEDE A-A

30800

2450 | 2600 | 1600 | 5600 | 6300 | 5600 | 1600 | 2600 | 2450

VOETPAD | FIETSPAD | RIJWEG | TRAMBAAN | RIJWEG | FIETSPAD | VOETPAD
HELLING 1:50 | HELLING 1:50 | | HELLING 1:50 | HELLING 1:50

6600 | 19800 | 6600

DOORSNEDE B-B

2750
3000

DOORSNEDE C-C

Bridge deck, schematic drawings

60 BRIDGE DECK & STAY CABLES

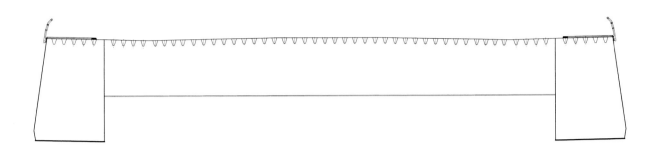

DOORSNEDE E-E

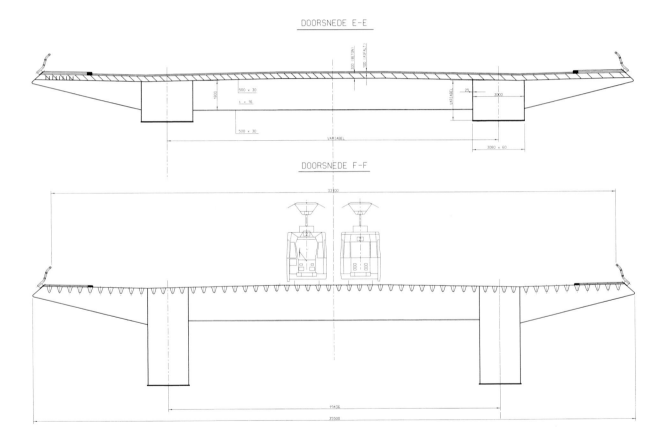

DOORSNEDE F-F

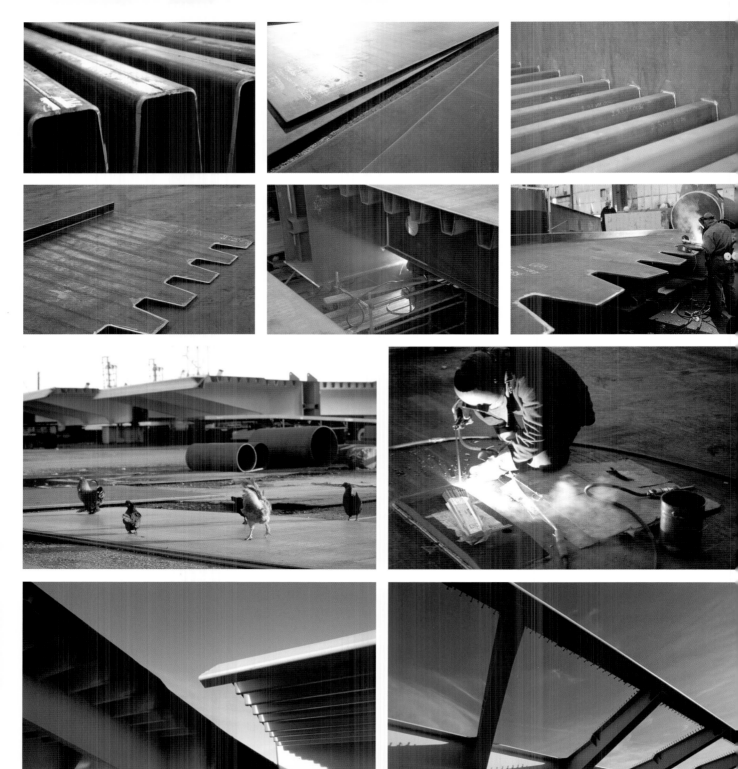

"At Heerema, they knew a lot about how certain components should be detailed. In particular, they knew in advance how large sections of the structure would behave when joined and during welding. They knew that you really could cut the plates with the aid of the computer and that they would fit perfectly." J. Reusink, *Chief Constructor, Steel Work, Rotterdam Public Works Department*

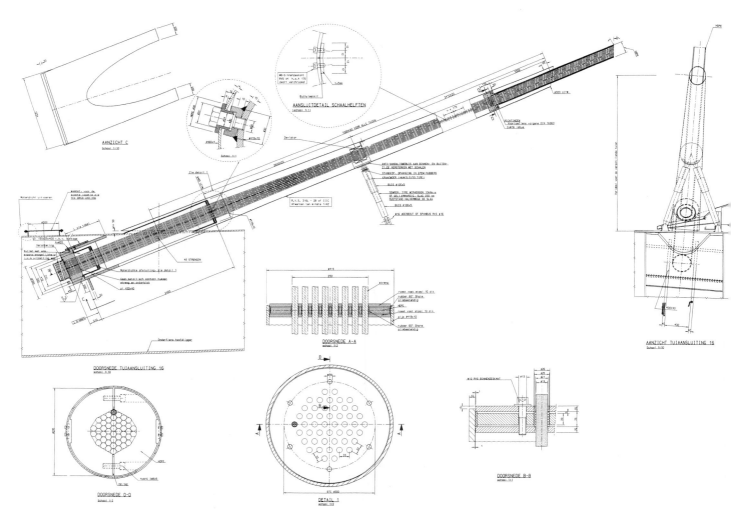

Construction drawings

"The plates for the cable anchorings are ten centimeters thick. A plate like that is a meter wide and some are room height—about two and a half to three meters. In terms of welding, that means eight square centimeters of welding. Calculated over a length of one meter, that comes to 800 cubic centimeters. A welder does about fifty cubic centimeters and hour, so that makes sixteen hours of welding in a one-meter joint like that. The welding was done from two sides so it took eight hours to make a single joint."

K. Noorlander, *Chief Constructor, Steel Work, Rotterdam Public Works Department*

above: Stay-cable strands

below: Unrolling metal strands

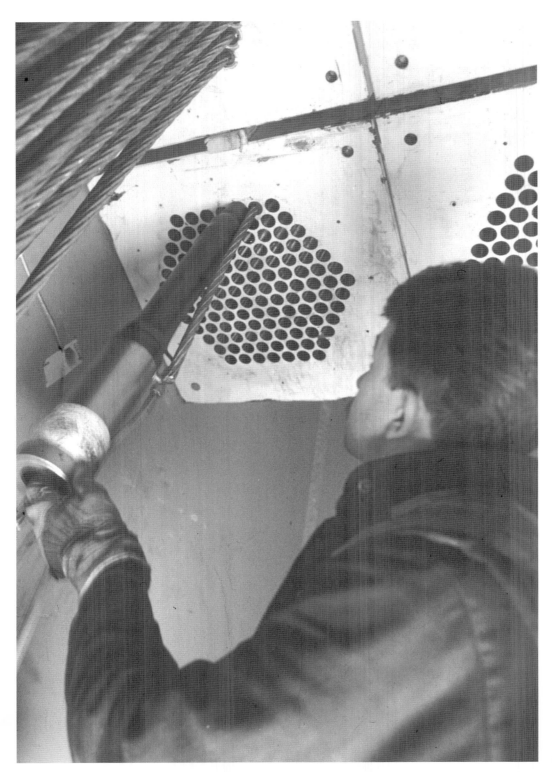

Stay-cable installation

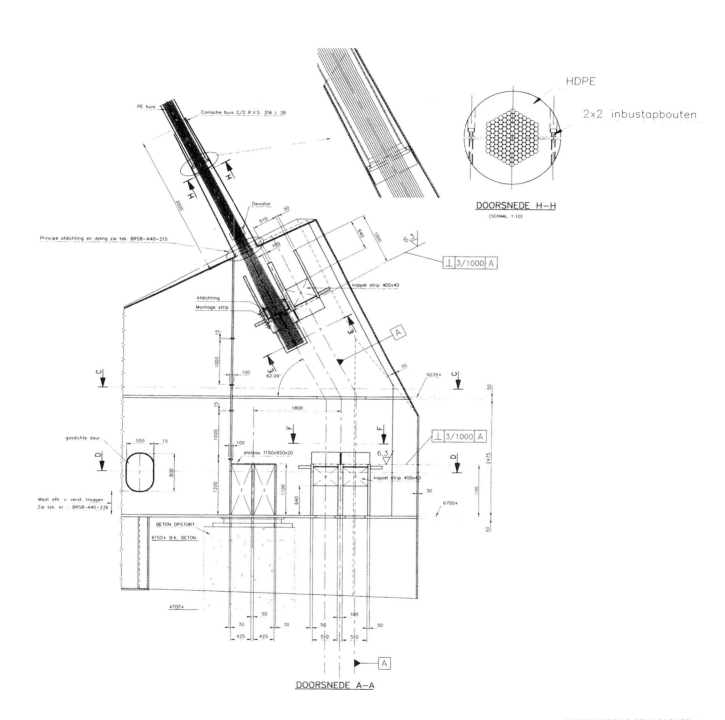

HDPE

2×2 inbustapbouten

PE buis

Conische buis 2/2 R.V.S. 316 L 2B

Deviator

Principe afdichting en deling zie tek. BRS8-A40-215

Afdichting

Montage strip

koppel strip 400x40

DOORSNEDE H-H
(SCHAAL 1:10)

⊥ 3/1000 A

gasdichte deur

Maat afh. v. verst. troggen
Zie tek. nr. : BRS8-A40-236

plateau 1150x920x20

koppel strip 400x40

BETON OPSTORT
6150+ B.K. BETON

⊥ 3/1000 A

9235+

4700+

6700+

DOORSNEDE A-A

Back stay anchor, detail

Stay-cable installation

Stay-cable connection at pylon

Assembly of deck sections on site

BvB: In order to maintain the wide vistas to the north of Noordereiland, we labored to keep the deck profile as thin as possible. Loads are carried internally by two steel box girders, 2.25-by-1.25 meters wide, which run the length of the bridge. The automobile and tram lanes occupy the center span, while the bicycle and pedestrian lanes cantilever from each side. The cantilever allowed us to narrow the profile at the edge even further, giving the illusion of greater thinness.

A different contractor, Smit Tak, constructed the bridge deck, also in a remote location. It was built in twenty-two fifteen-meter sections, which were then shipped to the site by barge. As each section was installed, the tension on the cables had to be adjusted to keep the bridge in equilibrium. With five sections positioned, enough load was in place to allow for the removal of the temporary support. The backstay strands were added sequentially with each additional section, until the entire span was negotiated.

Construction of bridge deck,
stay cables in foreground

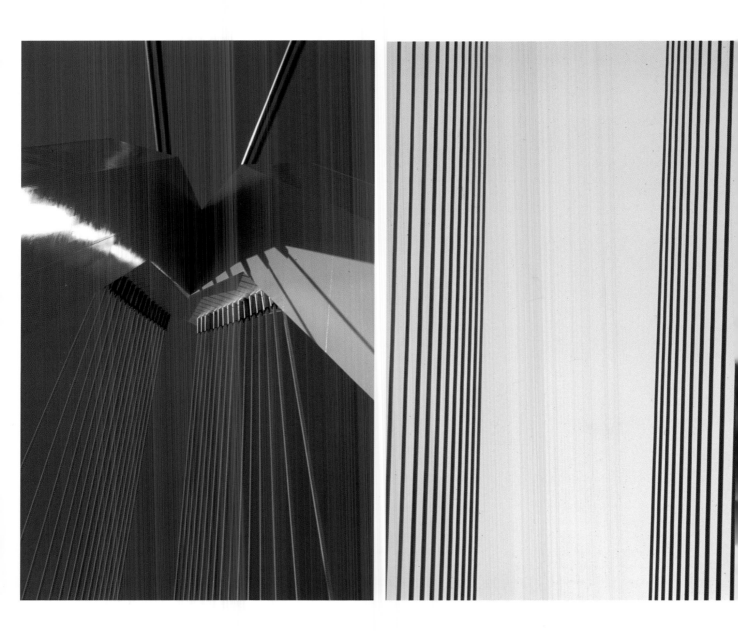

Stay cables

Stay cables

Stay cable, details

Stay cables
at night

BASCULE BRIDGE

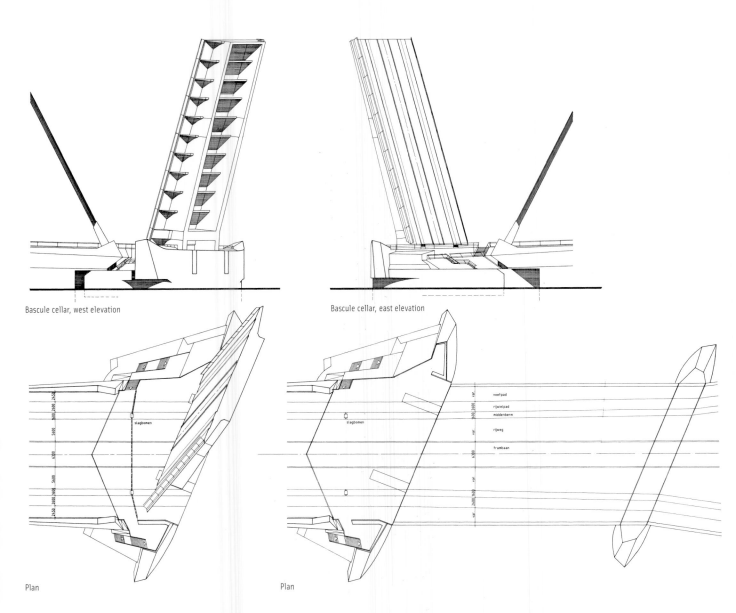

Bascule cellar, west elevation

Bascule cellar, east elevation

Plan

Plan

Bascule bridge, schematic drawings

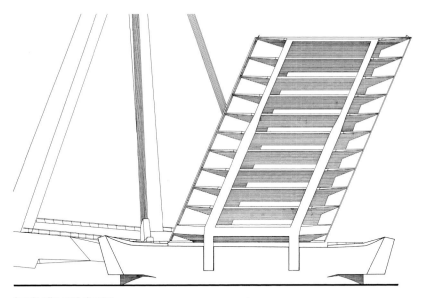

Bascule cellar, south elevation

BvB: The engineers were most enthusiastic about working on the bascule bridge, which was a far more complicated problem to solve. The main span allows 12.5 meters for shipping clearance, but in order to allow larger ships to pass, a lift bridge was required. This was an enormous project in itself. A fifty-five-meter passage was required, which we proposed to span with a single section. The difficulty resulted not from the span, however, but from the eccentric loads that resulted from the angle at which the shipping lane crosses the bridge. Due to its angled configuration, the bridge section leans toward Noordereiland when raised, concentrating the loads to one side. The calculations required were endless. Like the pylon, we modeled everything in the computer, with the resultant forces illustrated in color-coded drawings.

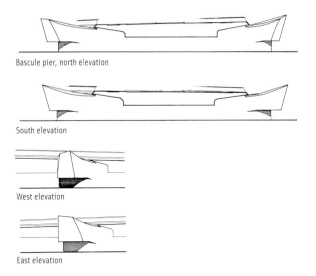

Bascule pier, north elevation

South elevation

West elevation

East elevation

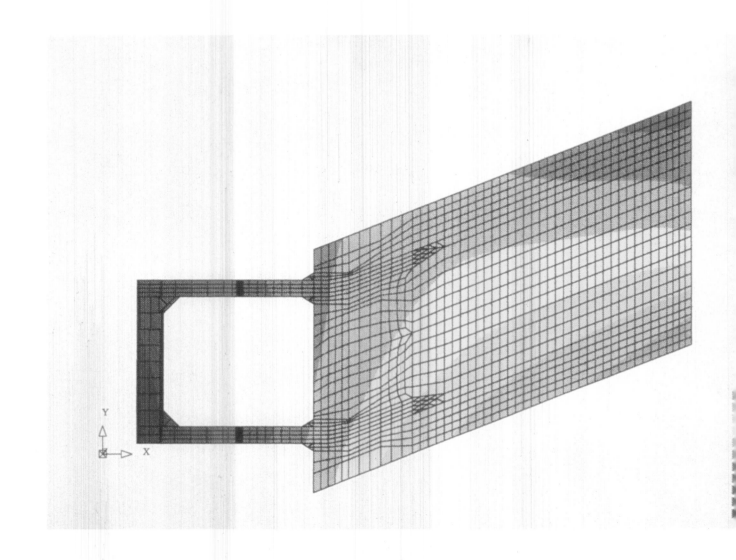

Structural force analyses of bascule bridge

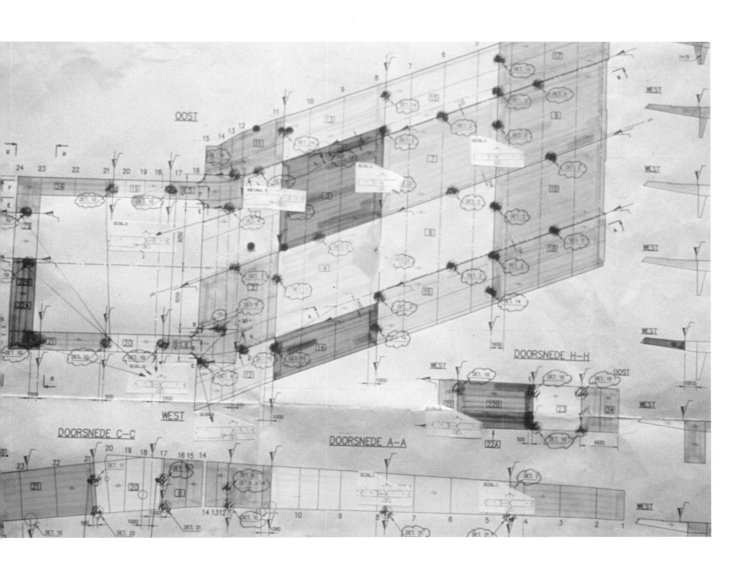

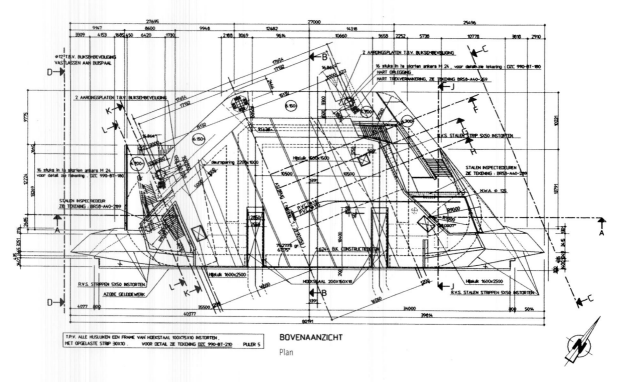

BOVENAANZICHT
Plan

Bascule cellar, construction documents

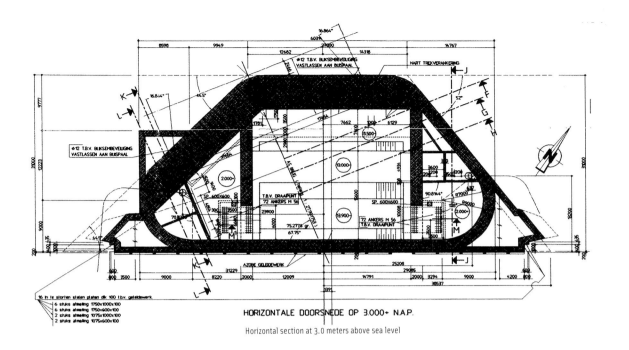

HORIZONTALE DOORSNEDE OP 3.000+ N.A.P.

Horizontal section at 3.0 meters above sea level

HORIZONTALE DOORSNEDE OP 8.000- N.A.P.

Horizontal section at 8.0 meters below sea level

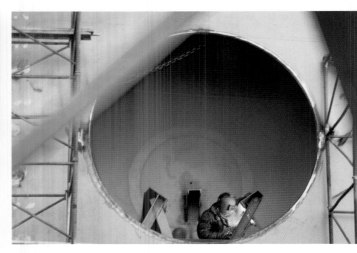

84 BASCULE BRIDGE

Installation of bascule machinery

above: Bascule caissons, formwork and reinforcing   *below*: Caissons

Bascule bridge
in open position

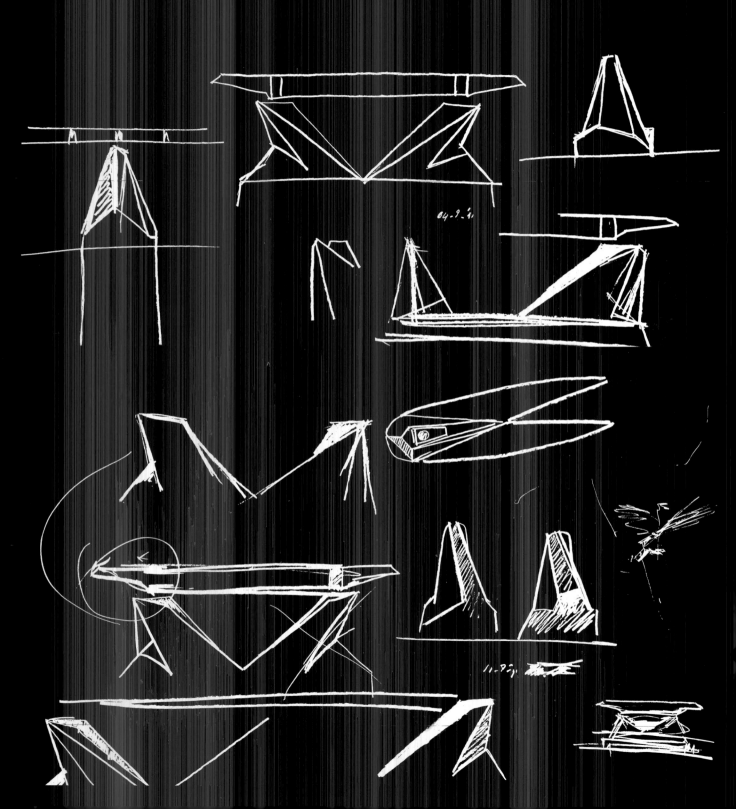

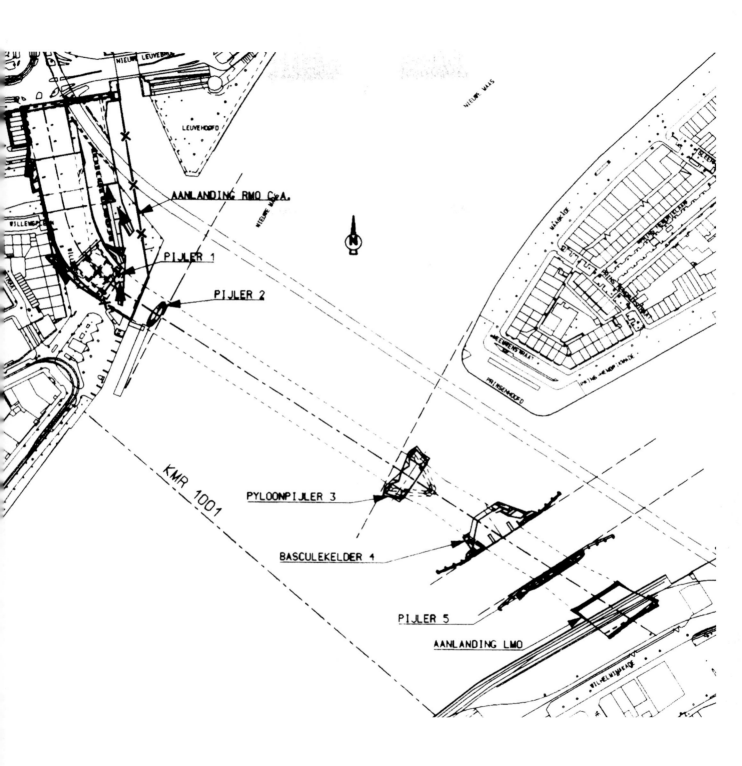

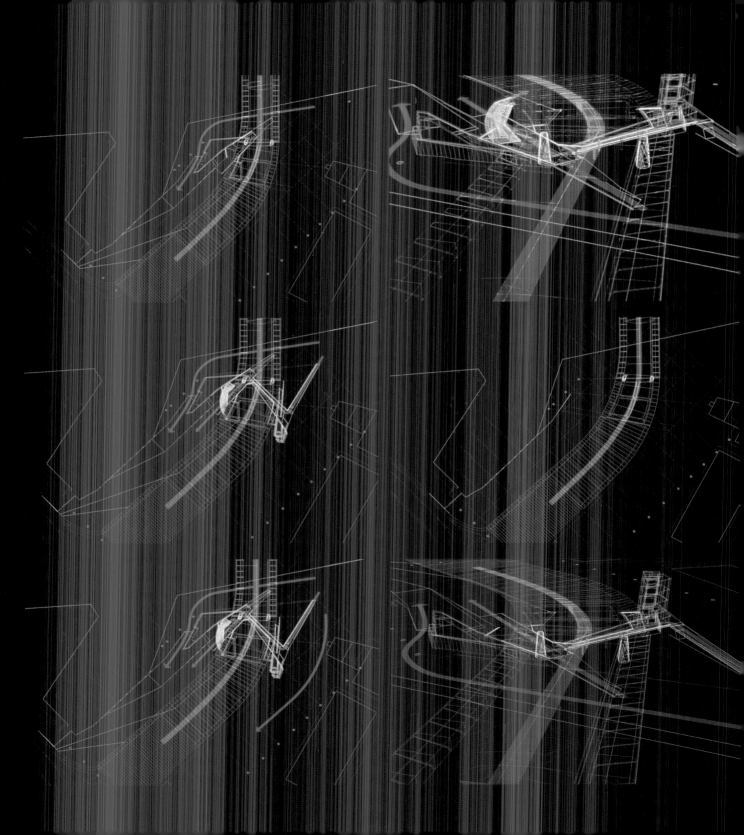

BvB: We were fanatical about the concrete work. We convinced everyone in the office that somehow the piers were more important than any other component of the bridge, even the pylon. As I mentioned earlier, this idea came from an interest in Brancusi. In his sculptures, the bases take on aspects of movement so important to the works themselves. In the Erasmus Bridge, we tried to achieve a similar effect—we wanted the piers to be inflected by the movement around them. They would appear to move with you.

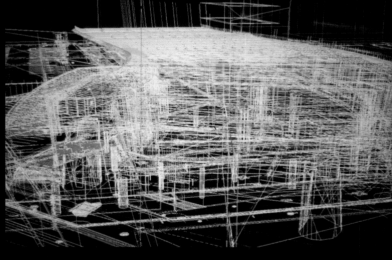

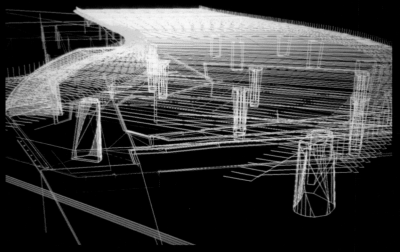

opposite: Site movement digrams with bridge piers and deck

left column and following spread: Views of wire-frame model at bridge landing

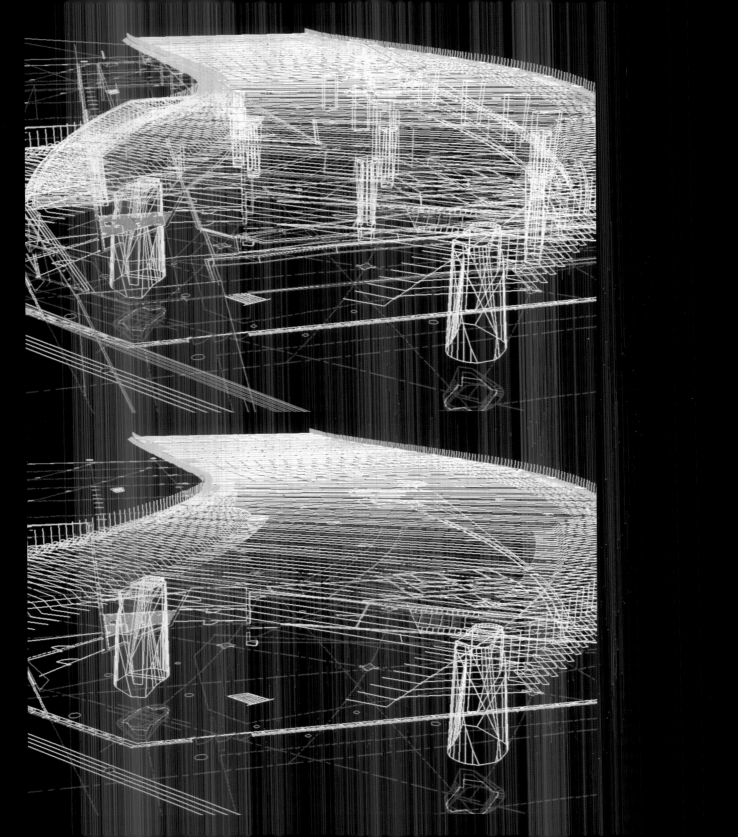

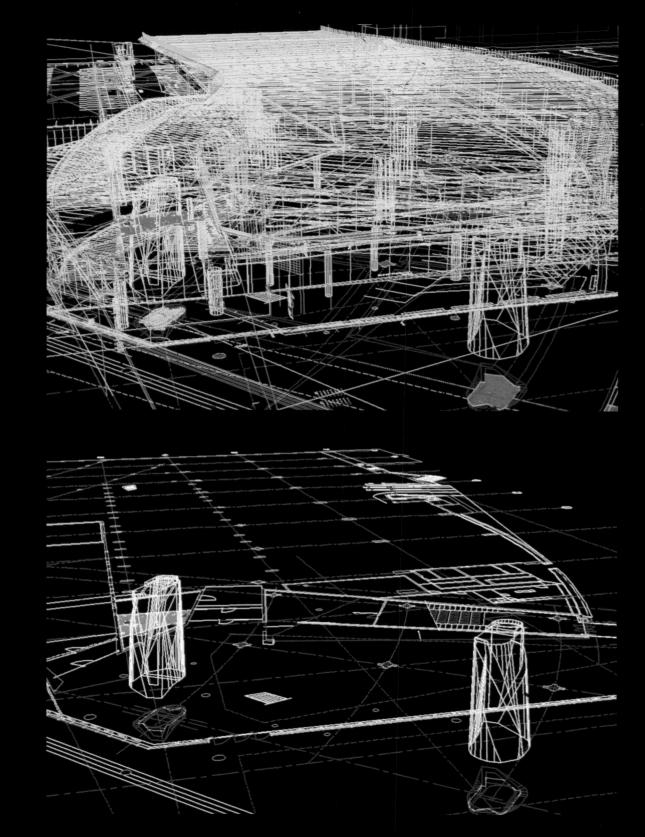

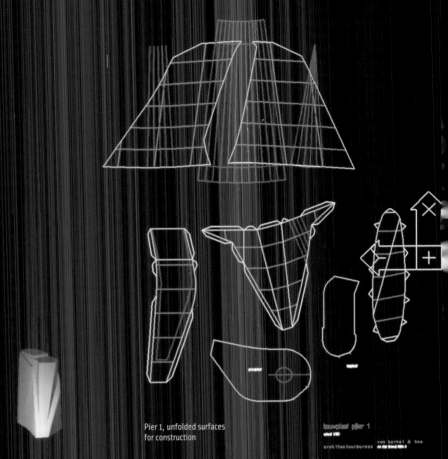

Pier 1, unfolded surfaces
for construction

bouwplaat pijler 1

wbad 1/10

van berkel & bos
architectuurbureau OK IN bemd) 100% B

Pier 1, rendered computer model

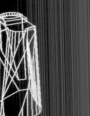

Pier 1, wire-frame computer model

We developed each pier using the computer, tracing the movements on the site across the structure of the bridge. Then we carefully modeled each pier in three dimensions. The structural loads were calculated by the engineers in a very straightforward manner and could be carried by the two cylinders seen in the wire-frame drawing. It was a give-and-take process, each step constituting a new layer in AutoCAD. We would design a support that took on the expressive form we were after, and then the engineers would tell us how the structural loads would be transferred through it. If the engineer's cylinder protruded through the envelope of our initial form, we would rework it to accommodate their requirements. The final design took into account all the forces at play, both expressive and structural.

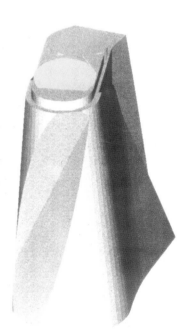
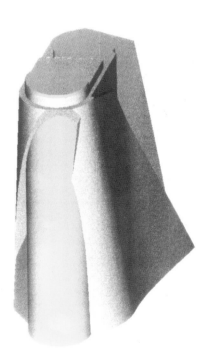
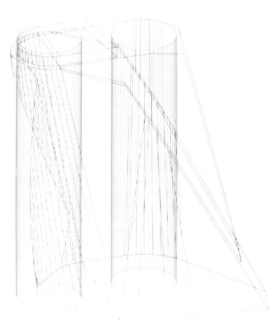

Pier 1, rendered (left and center) and wire-frame (right) computer models with required structure shown as yellow cylinders

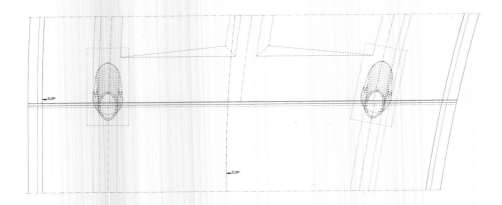

Pier 1, plan

Pier 1, north elevation

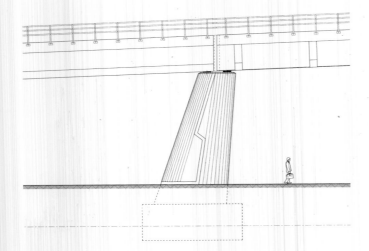

Pier 1, east elevation

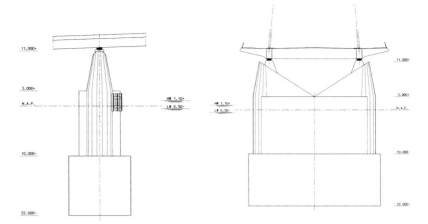

Pier 2, elevations

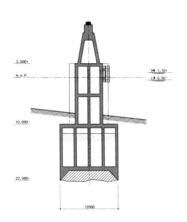

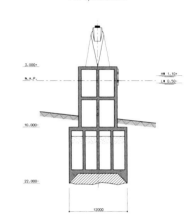

Pier 2, sections

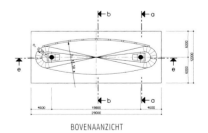

BOVENAANZICHT

Pier 2, plan

opposite and above:
Piers 1 and 2, preliminary
design drawings

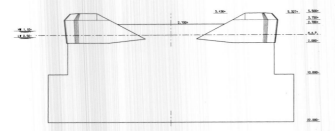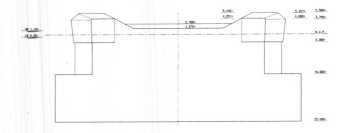

Pier 3, elevations

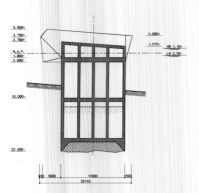

Pier 3, section

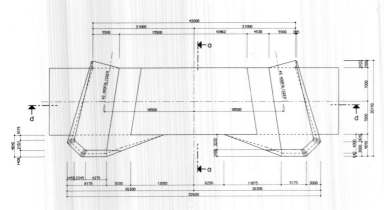

Pier 3, plan

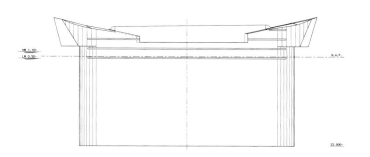

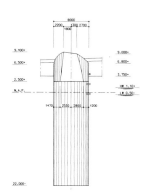

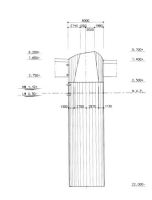

Pier 5, elevations

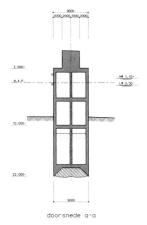

doorsnede a-a

Pier 5, section

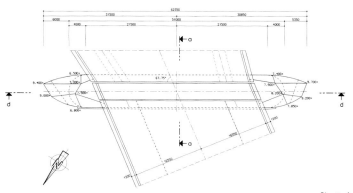

Pier 5, plan

opposite and above:
Piers 3 and 5, preliminary
design drawings

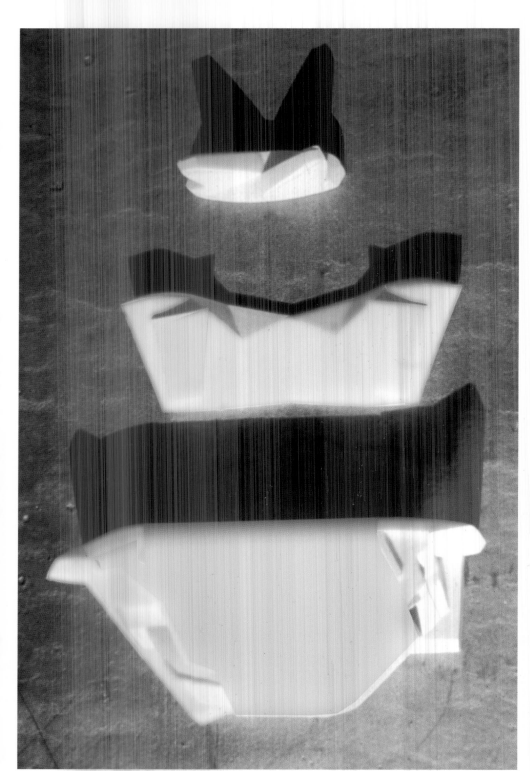

Pier 2

Pier 3

Pier 4, bascule cellar

Piers 2, 3, and 4, plaster models

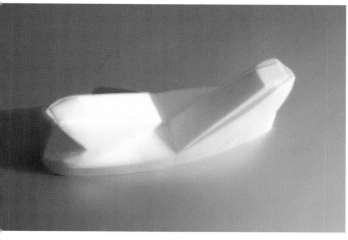

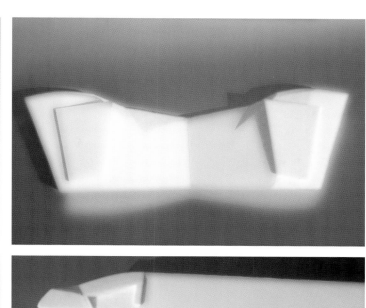

top right and left:
Piers 2 and 3, plaster models

bottom right and left:
Pier 4, bascule cellar,
plaster models

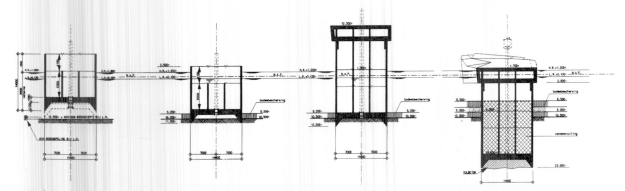

Pier 2, sections

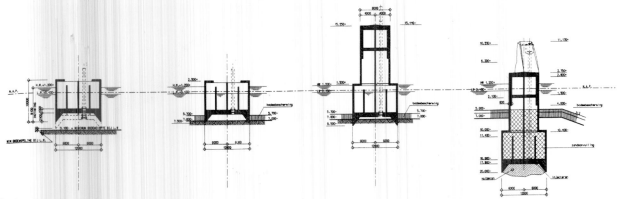

Pier 3, sections

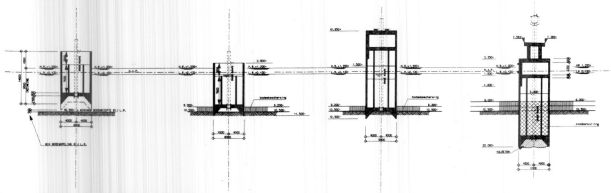

Piers 2, 3, and 5, line development of placement and construction

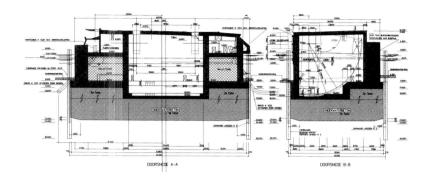

DOORSNEDE A-A   DOORSNEDE B-B

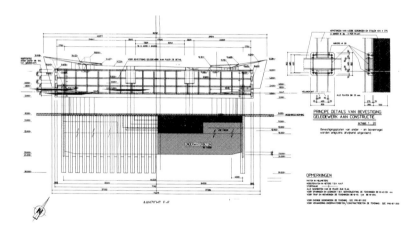

AANZICHT E-E

PRINCIPE DETAILS VAN BEVESTIGING
GELEIDEWERK AAN CONSTRUCTIE

OPMERKINGEN

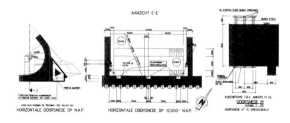

AANZICHT E-E

HORIZONTALE DOORSNEDE OP N.A.P.   HORIZONTALE DOORSNEDE OP 12.000- N.A.P.   DOORSNEDE M

Pier 4,
bascule cellar, sections

BvB: An enormous space was constructed below the surface of the river to house the counterweights and machinery for the bascule bridge. The space is housed within one of the five concrete piers, at the point where the backstays are anchored. The entire structure, resting on a nine-meter-thick base, was cast in place using underwater concrete. Once the structure was cast, the pit was drained and work on the machinery could begin.

Formwork, detail

Formwork, view from below

"The workmen are not used to making such complicated forms. The foreman needed more intensive guidance than for ordinary projects. Take the formwork, for example: in an ordinary job you oversee the first two compartments and the rest is just repetition. Here it's a different matter altogether. You can't use anything twice here, it's practically out of the question. Some of the walls slant one way, others slope in another direction. Even the car-park windows aren't rectangular." Z. Losonczi, *Works Foreman for CFEMBG, Contractor*

opposite, left: Formwork, detail

opposite, right: View showing bascule passage bumpers

While the bascule cellar was cast in place, the other piers located in the river were built as prefabricated caissons. The substructure was cast in Antwerp and then floated to the bridge site, where it was sunk into position.

The concrete firm had difficulty producing the formwork for the bridge piers, so, in the end, we produced the formwork drawings for them. This was also carried out in AutoCAD, in which we devised a method of unfolding the three-dimensional form into its two-dimensional components. From here, we solved the connections required and produced large-scale templates from which the forms were constructed.

This wood formwork, now all lost, was incredibly beautiful. It was a shame for it to go. But we designed the bumpers at the bascule passage in heavy timber and with the same intensity, so there remains a trace of the incredible carpentry work that went into the project.

View at water level, piers beyond

"I think without the computer we could never have made the formwork. Pier 1, or the steps that we're pouring now, for instance [stair 2], have all been realized with the help of the computer. The formwork drawings were worked out on the computer and then plotted out full size. After that, they were pasted to the wood boards in the factory and cut out with a fret saw."

K. Portengen, *Site Foreman, Rotterdam Public Works Department*

"The caissons for all the piers were made in Antwerp and transported to Rotterdam. Then we set them up as far as the architectural section which was very complicated in design. The thing was that the architect had also worked out the arrangement of the plate joints. This was so difficult that we couldn't make the forms on site. All the angles of the formwork were drawn three dimensionally with x, y, and z coordinates. We plotted the formwork on dry land— it's easier to work there. You're not on the river, on the caisson. Then we used a crane to move it all to the caisson. The various sections were so accurate that the whole thing fit exactly."

Z. Losonczi, *Works Foreman for CFEMBG, Contractor*

Formwork at pedestrian stair

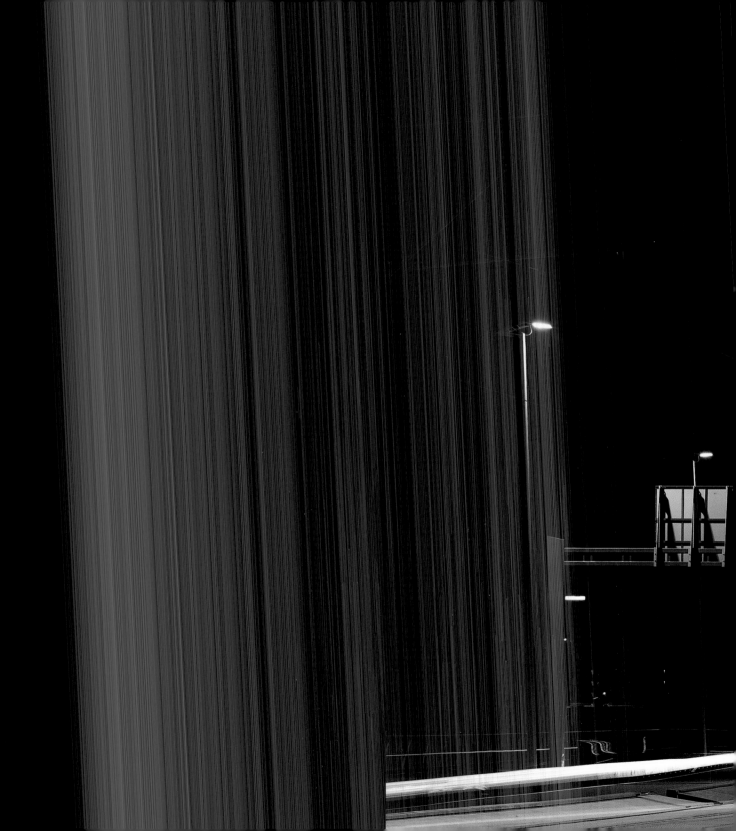

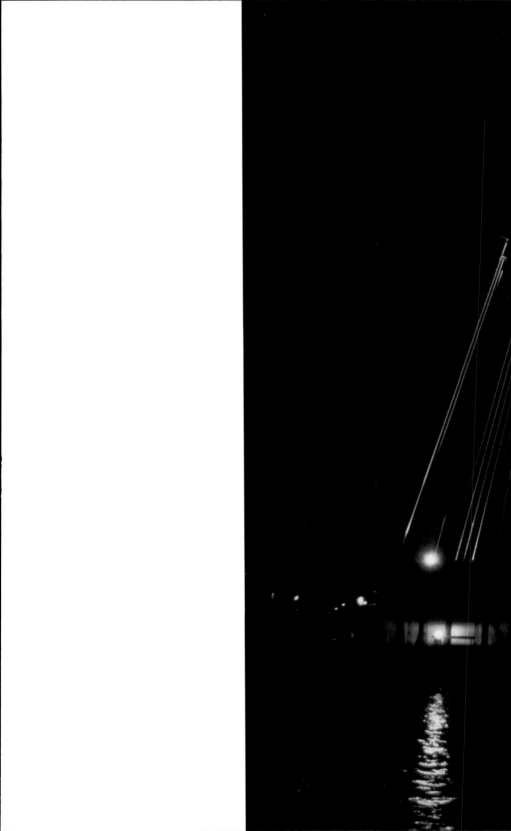

"Van Berkel's design was an attempt to render the symbolic value of the bridge as much as possible in its form. I think he succeeded 100 percent on this. On the other hand, only time will tell whether that symbolic aspect will be fully exploited. For my part, the test is whether the bridge will also prove attractive to slow-moving traffic. Will cyclists and pedestrians venture to use it? That's something the Williams Bridge never managed to bring off, by the way. I think it's going to work and that would be proof positive that it's possible to establish a relationship between the two parts of the city on this spot." J. Linthorst, *former Alderman responsible for the Rotterdam Physical Planning Department*

ed. note: The statement above was made in 1996. Since its opening, the bridge has accommodated consistently high volumes of pedestrian and bicycle traffic.

"The long and short of it is that we have discovered the river. Until then we had always seen the river as an artery over which goods flowed but which was not actually part of the city. Now we've discovered that instead of being a dividing line, the river could act as a link that would draw the two shores together. Only when you have discovered that binding effect can you start to think about extending the city to the other shore." Bram Peper, *Mayor of Rotterdam*

TG: *Mobile Forces* was produced concurrently with the Erasmus Bridge. It seems to me that publication remains crucial to the working of the practice. The books give you a place to test and clarify ideas—to codify them in anecdotal shorthand, as we see with Corporal Compactness or the Crossing Point. I see in your work a constant dialog between what you write and what you build; a symbiotic relationship exists in which it seems that one could not exist without the other.

BvB: It's interesting that you say that. I've never thought that we "have to do it" but maybe you are right. In fact, many artists seem to work in this way. We constantly find ourselves fascinated and obsessed with topics outside the projects we work on from day to day. In the books, we find a means for intermingling these outside ideas with our own work.

You might say that the books are self-reflective mirrors that chart a trajectory we would hope to follow in future works. It is one more component in this reconfigured practice toward which we aspire.

I think architects should try to be clairvoyant and books can help in that respect. They can outline a line of research to pursue and guide your direction. It is like making a diary. You outline a project, and then you do it.

TG: Do you think of the books as tools to drive the design forward or are they works in and of themselves?

BvB: They are definitely not works. For me they are nothing more than a machine for propelling design ideas.

TG: So we could think of a publication as yet another design technique?

BvB: Yes. It is a tool that can be used to draw people back into the work itself—it provides another angle of approach. The book holds the possibility of creating a fascination with the project in a totally new way.

TG: We might say that the most successful book in these terms would be one that makes people think, "I have to go to Rotterdam. I must see these effects for myself."

BvB: That would certainly make a successful book, but it could never be the project itself. In the end, the real test is the architecture.

ANIMATE URBANISM:
THE METABOLIC INFRASTRUCTURES OF UN STUDIO
Todd Gannon

*The reliance on erudition alone leaves postmodernism
in the same relation to architecture as female
impersonation to femininity. It is not architecture,
but building in drag.*
    Reyner Banham

Even the most inattentive observation of architects
and Americans confirms Dutch architect Winy Maas's
oft-quoted remark that architects use the word "landscape" as often as Americans use the word "fuck." From
Yokohama's new port terminal to Toronto's Tree City,
landscape is all the rage today, and as far as Americans
are concerned, well, fuck. But both groups possess
slightly broader vocabularies, and further investigation
reveals another popular pair of words: infrastructure
and shit.

In the context of the present essay, this coupling
is not accidental. For much of the twentieth century,
and despite important work by practitioners and critics
ranging from Rogers and Piano to Reyner Banham,
architects have treated infrastructure with a level of
disdain comparable to that usually reserved for its scat-
ological counterpart. The profane accommodation of
urban flows, whether traffic and sewage or power and
data, has been the business of engineers. Only recently
have infrastructural issues been readmitted into polite
architectural conversation, owing in large part to the
work of UN Studio, the Amsterdam-based office of Ben
van Berkel and Caroline Bos.

This newfound concern for infrastructure marks a pro-
found shift after forty years of more abstract architectural thinking. In the 1960s and 70s, opportunities
to build were rare for young practitioners and promi-
nent members of that generation, Eisenman, Tschumi,
Libeskind, and others, explored instead the isolated
autonomy of theoretical writing and paper architecture.
Major commissions such as the Wexner Center, Parc
de la Villette, and the Jewish Museum came later, after
world economies had rebounded and stellar reputations
had been forged.

By contrast, UN Studio (originally know as Van Berkel
and Bos Architectuurbureau) secured a number of
commissions soon after its founding in 1988. Early
projects include the typical fare of boutique practices—
international competitions, gallery installations, and
private residences—but it was the firm's embrasure
of utilitarian work, from low-profile power substations
to the world-famous Erasmus Bridge, that launched
UN Studio into the architectural spotlight. Van Berkel
and Bos's continued pursuit of infrastructural work,
combined with their frequent writings and teachings
on the subject, has cemented their reputation within
the discipline, making good on the ancient alchemical
dream of turning shit into gold.[1]

Infrastructure operates below the level of attention. This vital equipment heats and cools our homes and illuminates our streets and offices. It transports fuels, waste, goods, and all of us and delivers unknowable amounts of data to any point on the globe. Yet we scarcely notice it, for infrastructure performs its tasks anonymously, plying its effects subliminally. Whether at the scale of a building or at the scale of a city, it is most often found in the poché within walls or below grade, as if its mysterious functions were best carried out in secret. The marionette strings of the contemporary metropolis, infrastructure gives life to inanimate matter. Its reward is near total effacement.

This performative silence is required because architecture, as codified and practiced over the last two centuries, has been concerned first and foremost with signification. As the discipline repositioned itself within the Academy after centuries of close alignment with craft and building traditions, its attention shifted from problems of construction and accommodation to problems of aesthetics and representation.[2] Fashionable architects busied themselves with increasingly arcane stylistic experimentation, delegating responsibility for newly developed mechanical and electrical systems to a growing number of technical specialists. Today, plumbers,

engineers, and IT professionals continue to ensure that our buildings run smoothly, but for architects, superior functionality has never been enough. Architecture, we have all been taught, has to mean something.

Meaning is best inscribed under controlled conditions. The contingencies of movement, temporality, and function tend to create unwanted feedback that clouds the legibility of form. Recall Colin Rowe and Robert Slutzky's analysis of Le Corbusier's Villa Stein at Garches.[3] Here, the house is considered as abstract form, a collection of two-dimensional configurations represented in architectural drawings. Rowe and Slutzky uncovered an incredible range of compositional readings at Villa Stein, but this legibility came at a price. As oblique views would radically alter the subtle effects they found, the critics had to sacrifice (or at least postpone) direct experience of the architecture to enjoy them, apparently confining themselves to a fixed point in the garden, well away from the house itself.[4] In truth, their astute readings were likely not devised at Garches at all. Proving that critical distance can be quite substantial, Rowe and Slutzky probably developed their analysis over a desk at the University of Texas, studying plans and elevations.

Design methodologies reliant upon this combination of close attention and critical distance—the quotations of PoMo, the destabilizations of Deconstruction, the nostalgia of the New Urbanism—continue to hold sway over much of architectural theory and practice. But as pointed out by Stan Allen, "An architecture that works exclusively in the semiotic register and defines its role as critique, commentary, or even "interrogation" (laying bare of the intricacies of architecture's complicity with power and politics) has, in some fundamental way, given up on the possibility of ever intervening on that reality. Under the dominance of the representational model, architecture has surrendered its capacity to imagine, to propose, or to construct alternative realities."[5]

Infrastructural projects offer the opportunity to reclaim that capacity. To deal in bridges, tunnels, and highways is to operate directly on the material life of the city. No mere representation, infrastructure choreographs the experience of the city, plying effects more potent than any single building could muster. History provides ample evidence. The Greeks elevated the arts as never before, but the Romans took over the world. Aqueducts and roads affect everyone. Erudition, however formidable, plays to a much smaller crowd.

On the surface, UN Studio's projects bear a striking resemblance to the work of semiotic practices, and many critics have explored their representational and expressive effects.[6] Even Van Berkel and Bos's own writings reveal a concern for signification. Regarding the Erasmus Bridge they write, "while deriving from a commission too complex to view entirely in this light, [the bridge] is generated by an intricate system of references to and deviations from typologies from the surroundings."[7] Demonstrating an uncommon ability to operate effectively in both discursive and performative modes, the firm does not abandon the semiotic register, but rather deploys meaning as one of many effects in its arsenal. In recent projects, the manipulation of information remains a key component in their design process, though the legibility of that information in the final form is not a concern.[8] Instead, we see a persistent drive toward new possibilities of experience.

In his book *Investigations*, theoretical biologist Stuart Kauffman builds upon Charles Darwin's theory of evolution to explore the development of life in the universe. "The core issue," he explains, "arises with what Darwin calls 'preadaptations,' namely, causal consequences of parts of organisms that were not of adaptive significance in the normal environment of the organism, but might come to be of adaptive significance in some future environment and end up being selected for by natural selection. Thus arose hearing, lungs, flight—virtually all major and probably most or all minor adaptations."[9] New forms of life arise not through reactive adaptation to a context, but rather through "emergence and persistent creativity," generating what Kauffman refers to as "new possibilities for making one's way in the world."

In Kauffman's view, life starts out simply, the product of randomly-occurring chemical reactions.[10] Over time, the complexity of these chemical combinations increases, and the world (or body, or biosphere, or universe, or legal system, or economy) grows more diverse. This diversity gives rise to new forms of work (i.e., metabolism and photosynthesis) and new forms capable of doing that work (i.e., animals and plants). Further, the process of doing all this work affects the environment, creating additional "jobs" to be exploited.[11] In this model, an environment and its inhabitants co-construct one another, operating with equal impact on the infrastructural systems of bodies and biospheres as on the formal extravagances of fin, fur, and feather.

Applied to urbanism, Kauffman's insights accommodate the formal inventiveness of UN Studio's work as well as its affective potential on the city. Bridges, tunnels, and train stations, along with the proliferation of transportation, communication, and information networks, are the organs and metabolic processes that give life to the metropolis. The spectacular forms of the Erasmus Bridge, the Piet Hein Tunnel, or Arnhem Centraal, derived from the complex forces (political, representational, temporal, infrastructural) at play in the contemporary city, are not abstract representations of those forces but rather, like Kauffman's chemical reactions, the material manifestation of new forms of urban life. With them, Van Berkel and Bos chart a course away from the critical distance of semiotic practice toward an engaged, performative approach in which architecture once again operates directly on the ecology of the contemporary metropolis. These contorted forms and luxurious surfaces are the plumage of a new beast on the urban landscape. Their effects point to new possibilities for architects, allowing us to leave behind our role as commentators and to undertake the greater task of shaping new forms of life for the twenty-first century.

[1] See Dominique Laporte, *History of Shit* (Cambridge: MIT Press, 1993); originally published as *Histoire de la merde: prologue* (Paris: Christian Bourgios, 1978).

[2] Reyner Banham places the date of this rift between "the art of architecture and the practice of making and operating buildings" in the mid-eighteenth century. See Reyner Banham, *The Architecture of the Well-tempered Environment* (Chicago: Univ. of Chicago Press, 1969), 9.

[3] Colin Rowe and Robert Slutzky, "Transparency: Literal and Phenomenal," *Perspecta* 8: The Yale Architectural Journal, 1964. Reprinted in Todd Gannon, ed., *The Light Construction Reader* (New York: Monacelli Press, 2002), 91–101.

[4] As noted by Detlef Mertins. See his "Transparency: Autonomy and Relationality," *AA Files* 32, 1996. Reprinted in *The Light Construction Reader*, 137.

[5] Stan Allen, "Infrastructural Urbanism," in *Points + Lines: Diagrams and Projects for the City* (New York: Princeton Architectural Press, 1999), 50.

[6] See, for example, Bart Lootsma, "Ambidexterity and Transgression," and John Biln, "Lines of Encounter," both in Kristin Feireiss, ed. *Ben van Berkel: Mobile Forces* (Berlin: Ernst & Sohn, 1994). See also Greg Lynn, "Forms of Expression: The Proto-functional Potential of Diagrams in Architectural Design," in *El Croquis* 72 (1995), and Jeffrey Kipnis, "Hybridizations," in *A+U* 256 (1995).

[7] Ben van Berkel and Caroline Bos, "Mobile Forces," in Feireiss, *Ben van Berkel: Mobile Forces*, 29.

[8] For a specific discussion of legibility in UN Studio's work, see Jeffrey Kipnis, Steven Holl, Ben van Berkel, Caroline Bos, Jaques Herzog, and Rafael Moneo, "Discussion 3" in Cynthia Davidson, ed., *Anything* (Cambridge: MIT Press, 2000), 124–29.

[9] Stuart Kauffman, *Investigations* (London: Oxford University Press, 2000).

[10] A biosphere "construct[s] itself up from sunlight, water, and a small diversity of chemical compounds . . . over evolutionary time" (Kauffman, 82). For Kauffman, life evolves by organizing a complex interplay between matter, energy, and information. Entities measure displacements from equilibrium from which work can be extracted, as when a cat smells a mouse (measures displacement), pounces on it, and devours it (extracts work). In this sense, a living being, or "autonomous agent," is simply a self-replicating entity that manipulates the environment on its own behalf.

[11] Think of the ecological complexity of the Pacific Northwest. As salmon swim upstream to spawn, elevation changes in rivers, caused by various geological occurrences, force the fish to jump from one level to the next. Salmon able to jump are more likely to get upstream to spawn than non-jumpers, thus jumping salmon are selected for. But the jumping salmon also catch the attention of hungry bears, and many of those fish wind up as lunch. Bears able to catch fish are better off than non-fishers, and the fishers, in turn, are also selected for. Returning once more to scyballic themes, bears shit in the woods. They also drag salmon carcasses there. Nourished by these rich fertilizers, local trees soar to great heights, providing ideal nesting places for various birds. The shade beneath the trees provides optimal homes for certain other flora and fauna, and so on.

CREDITS

PROJECT CREDITS

CLIENT
Department of Public Works
of the City of Rotterdam
Development Company
Rotterdam (OBR)

Bram Peper, Mayor

ARCHITECTS
Van Berkel and Bos
Architectuurbureau, Amsterdam

Ben van Berkel, Architect
Freek Loos, Project coordinator

PROJECT TEAM
Hans Cromjongh
Ger Gijzen
Willemijn Lofvers
Sibo de Man
Gerard Nijenhuis
Manon Patty Nama
John Rebel
Ernst van Rijn
Hugo Schuurman
Caspar Smeets
Paul Toornend
Jan Willem Walraad
Dick Wetzels
Karel Vollers

TECHNICAL CONSULTANTS

STRUCTURAL DESIGN
Arie Krijgsman,
Preliminary design

Department of Public Works
of the City of Rotterdam
(Ingenieursbureau
Gemeentewerken Rotterdam)

CONSTRUCTION DESIGN
Engineering Department
Concrete and Steel (IBS)
Engineering Department
Harbor Works (IH)
Engineering Department Road
and Water Management (IWG)

LIGHTING DESIGN
Lighting Design Partnership,
Edinburgh
Douglas Brennan, IALD
Andre Tammes, IALD

PROJECT MANAGMENT
Department of Public Works
of the City of Rotterdam
(Ingenieursbureau
Gemeentewerken Rotterdam)

Electricity Company
Rotterdam–Centrum (ENECO)

BUILDING CONTRACTORS

PYLON ASSEMBLY
Heerema Dock Installations,
Vlissingen

CABLE STAYED BRIDGE
Steel: Grootint, Dordrecht;
Compagnie d' Entreprises
CFE, Brussels
Concrete: Maatschappij voor
Bouwen Grondwerken, Antwerpen

BRIDGE DECK
Smit Tak, Rotterdam

STAYS AND STRANDS
Tensacciai and Redaelli, Milan

BASCULE BRIDGE
Ravestein-Noell, Deest

PROTECTIVE COATING
DCS, Ridderkerk

LIGHTING MANUFACTURER
Bega Lighting

Ben van Berkel." *Architecture and Urbanism* 256 May 1995): passim.

Ben van Berkel, 1990–1995." *El Croquis* 72:1 (1995): assim.

etsky, Aaron. "Holland's Hypermodernist." rchitecture 86, no. 3 (March 1997): 76–87.

rown, David. "Building Bridges." *World Architecture* 53 February 1997): 84–103.

eireiss, Kristin, ed. *Ben van Berkel: Mobile Forces.* erlin: Ernst und Sohn, 1994.

etting, Catrien. "Bridging the Gap." *Urban Land* 57, o. 12 (December 1998): 22–23.

ipnis, Jeffrey. "Hybridizations." *Architecture and Jrbanism* 256 (May 1995): 62–63.

ootsma, Bart. "Rotterdam, Entre deux rivers." Architecture d'Audjourd'hui 306 (September 1996): 90–93.

____. "Van Berkel & Bos: A Bridge for Rotterdam." Domus 788 (December 1996): 26–32.

____. *Super Dutch: New Architecture in the Netherlands.* New York: Princeton Architectural Press, 2000.

Loriers, Marie Christine. "Reasonable Imperatives." *Techniques et Architecture* (February–March 2000).

Lynn, Greg. "Conversations by Modem with Ben van Berkel." *El Croquis* 72:1 (1995): 6–15.

____. "Forms of Expression: The Proto-functional Potential of Diagrams in Architectural Design." *El Croquis* 72:1 (1995): 16–31.

Melet, Ed. "Erasmusbrug in Rotterdam." *Architect* 4 (November 1997): 20–25.

Negrini, Laura. "UN Studio, Ben van Berkel and Caroline Bos: A Research Process in Evolution." *Industria delle constuzioni* 343 (May 2000): 6–61

Pasveer, Erik. "Lessons in Orchestration: the Kop van Zuid in Rotterdam." *Archis* 10 (October 1996): 18–29.

Pavarini, Stefano. "L'erasmus Bridge a Rotterdam." *Arca* 73 (July–August 1993): 48–53.

Rodermond, Janny. "Tussen global en lokaal: Van Berkel and Bos over veranderende ontwerpcondities." *Architect* 27, no. 9 (September 1996): 56–61.

Schindler, Verena. "Anti-tradition im Experiment: Die ErasmusBrücke aks kristalline Selbstdarstellung der Stadt Rotterdam." *Archithese* 27, no. 3 (May–June 1997): 34–37.

Terry, Clinton. "City Under Influence." *Diadalos* 57 (September 1995): 126–131.

Webbers, Hans, et. al. *De brug: Gescheidenis, architectuur en kunst.* Rotterdam: NAI Uitgevers, 1996.

Wortmann, Arthur. "Transformationen in Rotterdam." *Baumiester* 93, no. 12 (December 1996): 30–35.

Van Berkel, Ben. *Ben van Berkel: Architect.* Rotterdam : Uitgeverij 010, 1992.

Van Berkel, Ben and Caroline Bos. *Delinquent Visionaries.* Rotterdam: [Ben van Berkel], 1993.

____. "The Erasmus Bridge, Rotterdam." *Architectural Design* vol. 67, no. 9–10 (September–October 1997): 84–87.

____. *Move.* Amsterdam: Goose Press, 1999.

Van Winkel, Camiel. "Don't Slam Doors." *Archis* 10 (October 1996): 18–29.

BIOGRAPHY

Todd Gannon is a lecturer in architectural theory
and design at the Knowlton School of Architecture
and a project designer at Acock Associates Architects
in Columbus, Ohio. Previous books include
Morphosis/Diamond Ranch High School, *The Light
Construction Reader*, and *Bernard Tschumi/Zénith
de Rouen*.

Knowlton School of Architecture
The Ohio State University

SOURCE BOOKS
IN ARCHITECTURE

4

Erasmus Bridge
Rotterdam, The Netherlands

Todd Gannon, Volume Editor

Series Editor
Todd Gannon

PRINCETON ARCHITECTURAL PRESS, NEW YORK

Published by
Princeton Architectural Press
37 East Seventh Street
New York, New York 10003

For a free catalog of books, call 1.800.722.6657
Visit our Web site at www.papress.com.

Editor: Linda Lee
Designers: Lorraine Wild and Robert Ruehlman

Special thanks to: Nettie Aljian, Nicola Bednarek, Janet
Behning, Megan Carey, Penny (Yuen Pik) Chu, Russell
Fernandez, Jan Haux, Clare Jacobson, Mark Lamster,
Nancy Eklund Later, Nancy Levinson, Katharine Myers,
Jane Sheinman, Scott Tennent, Jennifer Thompson,
Joseph Weston, and Deb Wood of Princeton
Architectural Press —Kevin C. Lippert, publisher

Library of Congress Cataloging-in-Publication Data
UN Studio : Erasmus Bridge / Todd Gannon,
volume editor.
p. cm. — (Source books in architecture ; 4)
ISBN 1-56898-464-2 (pbk. : alk. paper)
1. Erasmusbrug (Rotterdam, Netherlands) 2. Bridges-
Netherlands-Rotterdam- Design and construction.
3. UN Studio. I. Gannon, Todd. II. Series.
TG78.R68 E73 2004
624.2'3'09492385—dc22
                                        2003017224